BOAT ENGINES

A **Motor Boat & Yachting** Book

DICK HEWITT

FERNHURST BOOKS

First Published in Great Britain as a series of articles entitled
'Understanding Engines' in *Motor Boat and Yachting*, 1989; first
published in book form in 1990 by Fernhurst Books, Duke's Path,
High Street, Arundel, West Sussex BN18 9AJ

The publishers wish to thank *Motor Boat and Yachting* and Volvo
Penta UK for their assistance in publishing this book.

All pictures and diagrams were supplied by Motor Boat and
Yachting except the following: Rodger Witt, pages 28, 35 and 55.

Cover photo reproduced with permission of Sunseeker International
(Boats) Ltd

British Library Cataloguing in Publication Data
A catalogue record for this book is available from the British Library

ISBN 1 898660 04 2

Edited and designed by Joyce Chester
Typeset by Central Southern Typesetters, Eastbourne
Printed through World Print Ltd, Hong Kong

CONTENTS

FOREWORD

Any boat that has an engine needs somebody to love and cherish it. This book is addressed to that person – and to anybody else who may have charge of the boat from time to time.

Whether the engine is large or small, or of whatever type, it is first necessary to have some basic knowledge of how it functions. Only then can one begin to understand the need for the various maintenance tasks of a routine nature, or be able to identify any warning signals that the engine may show, or work out what has happened when it suddenly stops or refuses to start. It is worth observing that with a twin-screw boat there is double the work, and that statistically it is twice as likely that something will go wrong – so in that case you had better read the book twice as carefully!

I am grateful for the helpful contributions made by Tim Bartlett, the Technical Editor of *Motor Boat & Yachting* in which the series first appeared. I also acknowledge the kind assistance of various engine manufacturers, among them Volvo Penta UK Ltd, Perkins Engines Ltd, Sabre-Lehman and Outboard Marine (UK) Ltd.

Dick Hewitt

1. THEORY AND INSTALLATIONS

Marinisation – Performance – Power curves – Other methods of propulsion – Petrol and diesel engines compared – Methods of installation

Half a century ago or more, seagoing motor boats often carried auxiliary sails. Apart from their steadying effect, sails were a useful standby in the event of engine failure. Modern designs of motor cruisers hardly lend themselves to masts and sails, so today's skipper is even more dependent on the boat's engine or engines. Failure of the machinery is often just inconvenient, but if it happens at the wrong moment it can prove dangerous – even fatal.

Thus a skipper needs a sound knowledge of how an engine functions, what preventive maintenance is needed to keep it running smoothly, and what to look for when things go wrong. To achieve this he needs some understanding of what is actually going on inside an engine, and to know the function and relationship of the main working parts. Only then can he properly tackle the basic maintenance that is needed. By working around the engine he will learn more about its various components together with the systems (such as fuel, cooling, lubricating and exhaust) which are essential for its proper functioning. This will help when it comes to taking the right action to overcome any problem.

MARINISATION

Before starting to investigate the workings of the marine engines which power the majority of pleasure craft, it should be pointed out that most are not really marine engines at all. They are adaptations (marinisations is a longer but better word) of automotive or industrial units which have been made more suitable for marine use. But the characteristics of car and truck engines, which deliver their power at higher revolutions per minute (rpm) by means

of gearboxes with four speeds or more, are not at all suited to propelling a boat by a conventional screw propeller, because this implies a small propeller rotating at high speed. Such an arrangement is very inefficient, since a boat's propeller needs to be as large as can be arranged and to rotate more slowly. So these marinised units need suitable gearboxes to convert rpm into torque.

Engines driving cars or trucks very seldom run at or near their maximum rated power for any length of time, whereas it is possible for a boat engine to develop its maximum output continuously for hour after hour. So marinised engines are usually downrated by perhaps ten per cent, sometimes depending upon the particular application since the engines of pleasure craft are considered to receive lighter treatment than those in commercial vessels.

Other problems are posed by the use of materials which may not be very suitable in a marine environment, and by the different need for access to the machinery since a boat engine cannot be approached from the underside. So it is as well to be aware at the outset that the engine mariniser has several matters with which to contend, and that some produce a better answer than others. An engine marinised from the product of a major automotive manufacturer has the great advantage of spares being available from a worldwide dealer network.

PERFORMANCE

An engine will only drive a given hull at a certain speed, and it is useful to have an understanding of this relationship if only to avoid disappointment regarding a boat's performance. If you are intending

to fit a new or different engine to a hull it is important to have a complete grasp of this subject, or to
seek professional advice. But most owners have the
engine or engines which the designer has specified
for the boat concerned and can only hope that the
choice has been a good one. It will probably have
been determined largely by experience, but more
substantial craft will have been tank-tested as part
of the design.

For displacement craft – that is for hulls which
are driven through the water rather than skimming
over the surface – the maximum realistic speed
depends upon the square root of the waterline length
according to the formula:

$$V = 1.34 \times \sqrt{L}$$

where V is in knots and L is the waterline length in
feet. Thus where L is 36ft, the equivalent value of V
is 1.34 × 6, or 8 knots. The designer's art is to
provide an engine which will achieve that speed,
with a little power in hand to allow for rough water, a
head wind, a dirty bottom and some overloading.

Any further increase in power will not result in
any appreciable increase in speed due to the wave
system which the hull creates in moving through
the water. At the speed equivalent to 1.34 × √L
the boat is supported by a wave crest at the bow and
another at the stern. Any further increase in speed
moves the aft crest past the stern of the boat, so
that the stern slumps into the trough and the boat
is in effect trying to steam uphill, or more correctly
up the back of the transverse wave she is creating.
This is usually only achieved by boats with very
powerful engines, wide transoms and flat sections
aft that generate the necessary lift: planing craft.

Suitably designed boats with sufficiently powerful
engines can plane over the surface, with wave-making
resistance and the wetted area of the bottom both
greatly reduced, under conditions where V/√L may
be 2.5 or 3.0 or even more. Even then there is a
limit to the speed that can be achieved by a certain
power, approximately expressed in the formula:

$$\text{Speed} = K \times \sqrt{(bhp \div \text{Displacement})}$$

where speed is in knots and displacement is in
tons. The factor K depends on the hull form and

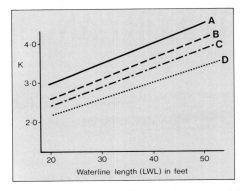

Fig 1. The constant K, used for calculating speed from
bhp and displacement for planing hulls, plotted against
waterline length.

the beam/length ratio, and can vary between about
2.25 and 3.85 for most planing craft with waterline
lengths between 20ft (6m) and 40ft (12m). Typical
values of K are shown in Fig 1 (with acknowledge-
ment to Perkins Engines) for four types of planing
craft as follows:

A: for shallow-vee hulls, with deadrise up to 10°,
and B/L ratios of 0.4 for 20ft lwl and 0.33 for 40ft lwl.
B: for moderate/deep-vee hulls, with deadrise greater
than 10°, and B/L ratios of 0.33 for 25ft lwl, and
0.25 for 40ft lwl.
C: for early shallow-vee hulls, with deadrise less
than 10° and B/L ratio about 0.20.
D: for round-bottom planing hulls, with fine bows
and wide flat sections towards the transom.

It should be noted that it is necessary to inter-
polate between the lines of the diagram for different
hull forms, and that the resulting figures for K may
prove somewhat pessimistic for modern planing
hulls with waterline lengths of less than about 25ft
(7.5m) and beam/length ratios of 0.4 or more.

POWER CURVES

The characteristics of an engine are shown by power
curves (see Fig 2) derived from running the engine
at full load on a test bed with a brake to measure
the torque developed at different speeds (rpm). From

the torque is calculated the power, the rate of doing work, which is expressed as horsepower (hp) or in metric units as kilowatts (kW):

$$1hp = 0.7457kW$$
$$1kW = 1.3410hp$$

The imperial unit of horsepower (hp) is almost the same as the metric unit of horsepower, which is described variously as a cheval-vapeur (CV) in France, a Pferdestarke (PS) in Germany, and a hast-kraft (HK) in Scandinavia:

$$1hp \text{ (Imp)} = 1.014hp \text{ (metric)}$$
$$1hp \text{ (metric)} = 0.986hp \text{ (Imp)}$$

Torque represents the thrust developed at different rpm, and is most easily described as a measure of the flexibility of a car engine – the ability to stay in one gear before changing down. It is important for the engines of planing craft or ski boats, where good acceleration is needed at relatively low rpm to get the boat on the plane or to pull a skier out of the water.

If all the various power consuming ancillaries are fitted, the power measured will be what the engine can deliver to the propeller shaft (at certain atmospheric temperature and pressure) and is called the shaft horsepower (shp). This is rather less than

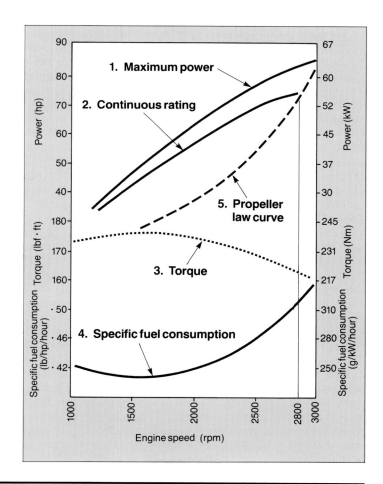

Fig 2. Power curves for a marine engine: (1) maximum (intermittent) rating; (2) continuous rating; (3) torque; (4) specific fuel consumption; (5) propeller law curve. All plotted against engine rpm.

the brake horsepower (bhp) measured without the ancillaries mentioned, so international standards are laid down for engine testing.

The power that an engine will develop at certain rpm is called rating, and two curves are shown in Fig 2 – one for the maximum intermittent power for a limited period (usually one hour in twelve) and the other for the continuous rating which can be developed indefinitely.

Sadly not more than about a third of the theoretical energy contained in the fuel that is burned is actually available at the propeller shaft as shp. About 10 per cent of the fuel's energy goes in driving the ancillaries already mentioned, about 30 per cent goes overboard as heat lost in cooling water, and about 30 per cent disappears with heat in the exhaust gases. Of the remaining 30 per cent not much more than half goes to driving the boat through the water.

Another curve shown is specific fuel consumption – the amount of fuel used per unit of power in unit time. As can be seen, the most economical running conditions correspond to the highest torque. The specific fuel consumptions of different types of internal combustion engines can vary a great deal, with medium-speed diesel engines having figures almost twice as good as two-stroke petrol engines used in outboards.

Power curves for marine engines usually include a propeller law curve, which is an estimate of the power that the propeller can absorb at different rpm. Where this meets the power curve represents the conditions under which the engine is generating maximum power. At lower speeds the engine is on part load, and the vertical distance between the propeller curve and the power curve shows the reserve of power that is available at that speed.

One way of getting more power from any given engine is to run it at a higher speed. Piston speed (in ft/min) is obtained by multiplying the stroke (in inches) by rpm and dividing by six, and is a good indication of the likely life of an engine. A healthy figure is about 1500ft/min, as found in slow-running marine diesels. Faster-running diesels, with better power/weight ratios, may have figures of 2000-2500ft/min, while for petrol engines the piston speed may be 3000ft/min or more. A single engine, driving a propeller on the boat's centreline, is the most efficient and most economical way of propelling a motor boat. For a given power output a single engine is cheaper to buy, cheaper to run, cheaper to maintain, lighter in weight, and takes up less space. However, high-speed boats may require a total power that can only be satisfied by providing two (or more) engines, and twin screws do bring the advantages of manoeuvrability and increased reliability provided they are installed as two independent units.

OTHER METHODS OF PROPULSION

In this book we shall be considering internal combustion engines powered by either petrol or diesel fuel. But it is right to mention that there are other possibilities – such as steam, which had its day in the last century. A number of enthusiasts still give loving attention to their steam boats, which have the great attraction of silent running, but the traditional boiler and engine are heavy and bulky items and it takes time to raise steam from cold.

Electric boats are also silent, as well as being cheap to maintain and easy to operate. As batteries are steadily improved to give an increasing number of charge/discharge cycles we may see more use of electric propulsion, which at present is confined to special situations where it is feasible to provide the necessary points for battery charging.

At one time paraffin was often used as an alternative fuel for internal combustion engines, because it was slightly cheaper and a bit safer than petrol. It was also then more universally available, which is not the case today. Paraffin is now out of favour on several counts. Firstly because it is necessary to start a paraffin engine on petrol, which means having two fuel systems. Then the compression ratio of a petrol-paraffin engine must be lower (about 7:1) which means that it generates less power. Thirdly, paraffin is rather a smelly fuel and its oily content means that the engine has to be decarbonised more often.

Nowadays on shore we are perhaps more gas-conscious than ever before, and internal combustion engines can be adapted to run on gases such as propane. The main disadvantage is that gas is not normally available in bulk at the waterside.

PETROL AND DIESEL ENGINES COMPARED

Having eliminated the competition, nearly all the propulsive units found in motor boats are internal combustion engines powered by petrol or diesel. Which is better depends largely on the particular application. Petrol engines have a better power/weight ratio, so their use may be dictated for small, high-speed boats. For a given power output they are not only lighter but cheaper, easier to maintain, less smelly, and quieter in operation. But petrol does have its disadvantages since it is more expensive and more dangerous to handle. Petrol engines also need electrical ignition systems which, although now more reliable than in the past, do not survive well with continuous exposure to damp and salty conditions.

So diesel engines are more reliable at sea, and are safer and cheaper to run. On the down side, they are more expensive, heavier, smellier, and noisier; and their important fuel injection equipment does need professional maintenance and scrupulously clean fuel.

Petrol engines are the more suitable for lighter, faster craft – fast runabouts and ski boats for example, and particularly in outboard engine form – or for auxiliary propulsion in smaller sailing yachts. Heavier craft, such as workboats and fishing boats, together with motor cruisers which require higher powers, are invariably driven by diesel units.

METHODS OF INSTALLATION

There are different ways that an engine can be installed in a boat, and there are different ways by which its power can be transmitted and put to use. In the conventional inboard installation (see Fig 3) the engine is mounted in the bottom of the hull, usually somewhere aft of amidships, and is connected directly to a gearbox. The gearbox allows ahead/neutral/astern operation to be selected as required, and it also often reduces the revolutions of the propeller shaft by a factor of about two, so that the propeller will work more efficiently. If the engine and the gearbox are flexibly mounted (to reduce hull vibration) the propeller shaft will be connected to the gearbox by a flexible coupling. A watertight sterngland is fitted in the hull where the shaft passes outboard to the propeller, and the aft end of the shaft is steadied by a water lubricated bearing held in what is known as an 'A' or 'P' bracket protruding from the bottom of the boat.

Fig 3. Conventional inboard engine installation, showing layout of gearbox and shafting: (1) engine; (2) gearbox with drop-centre transmission; (3) shaft coupling; (4) propeller shaft; (5) sterngland; (6) sterntube bearing; (7) shaft bracket; (8) propeller.

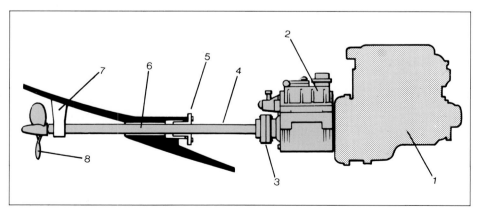

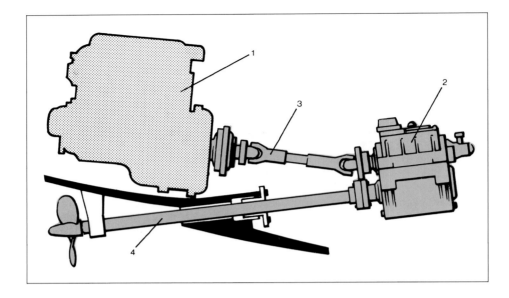

Fig 4. V-drive installation: (1) engine; (2) separate V-drive gearbox; (3) articulated shaft; (4) propeller shaft.

Such a layout has several advantages. The engine's weight is low down, and near the centre of the boat, while the space immediately above it can normally be used as the wheelhouse or cockpit. In a single-screw boat, with the engine and shafting on the centreline, the propeller is well immersed and nicely protected, although it should be noted that some single-engined fishing boats have the screw offset to one side so that the other side is clear for hauling nets or lines. Twin screws protrude on each quarter, and are therefore not so well protected. As an alternative to a gearbox, a controllable pitch propeller may be fitted for ahead/neutral/astern operation, but unless this is fitted to a slow-revving engine it is necessary to have some reduction ratio for efficient running.

Twin shafts are usually handed, with the propellers out-turning: in other words the starboard propeller, viewed from aft, turns in a clockwise direction, while the port propeller turns anti-clockwise. Out-turning propellers give better manoeuvring than in-turning ones. Often both engines rotate in the same direction, and the different rotation is achieved in one of the gearboxes.

If, for design reasons to do with the distribution of weight, it is necessary for the engine or engines to be installed further aft in the boat, then the engine can be reversed so that the drive is taken

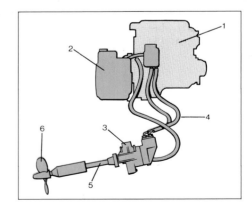

Fig 5. Hydrostatic drive: (1) engine, sited as convenient; (2) hydraulic pump; (3) hydraulic motor; (4) flexible pipes connecting pump to motor; (5) propeller shaft; (6) propeller.

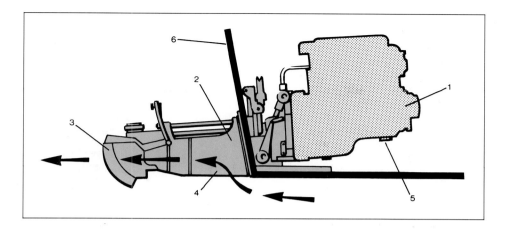

Fig 6. Water jet propulsion: (1) engine; (2) pump; (3) directional jet outlet; (4) water intake; (5) engine mounting; (6) transom. The arrows indicate water flow (ahead operation).

forward to a V-drive gearbox from which it is led aft like an ordinary propeller shaft, as shown in Fig 4.

Another form of installation is provided by a hydro-static drive, as in Fig 5. The engine is connected to a hydraulic pump, from which flexible pipes run to a hydraulic motor on the forward end of a short propeller shaft. This allows the engine to be fitted anywhere inside the hull, and minimises the problem of engine alignment, which makes installation easier. Control is simple, and power can be changed from full ahead to full astern without any damage, which is not the case with a conventional gearbox. However there is some loss of efficiency, which gets worse with the length of hose used.

In another installation a water jet replaces the normal propeller (see Fig 6). The engine drives a pump which draws in water through an intake in the bottom and forces it out at the stern, the result-ing reaction driving the boat. To be efficient, a jet unit needs to deal with large quantities of water at relatively low velocity, and the more powerful units may have two or even three impellers arranged in stages. Deflectors are used to direct the jet flow to steer the boat, and a bucket arrangement provides

excellent astern power. Since there is no propeller and shafting to protrude below the hull, jet units are ideal for shallow water operation and they are also safe for water skiing or rescue purposes. Instal-lation is easy because there is no shafting to line up, and there is not the drag which is caused by conventional shafting and shaft brackets.

Outdrives or sterndrives (see Fig 7) have a power unit mounted on the inside of the transom, through which a short horizontal drive shaft passes to the leg, or drive unit, on the outboard side. Bevel gears

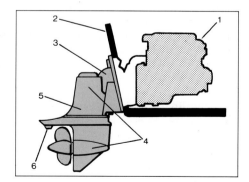

Fig 7. Outdrive installation: (1) engine; (2) transom; (3) universal joint between engine and top of vertical drive shaft, to allow steering and tilting; (4) bevel gears at the top and bottom of vertical drive shaft; (5) cavitation plate; (6) trim tab.

at the top and bottom of a vertical shaft within the leg transmit the power to a short propeller shaft at the bottom of the leg. Apart from changing the direction of drive through two right angles, the gears also incorporate ahead/neutral/astern operation and a reduction ratio. The leg swivels on a vertical axis to steer the boat by directing the thrust of the propeller. This gives very positive steering, provided that the propeller is rotating (either ahead or astern). The leg can also be raised to bring the propeller out of the water, which is useful either for access or if the boat has to take the ground. Almost all outdrives are fitted with power tilt and trim, which allow the leg to be raised or lowered mechanically. Minor alterations in trim change the direction of the propeller thrust in the vertical plane. Ideally this is used to keep the thrust horizontal,

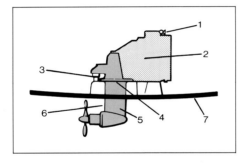

Fig 8. Sailboat (or S-) drive: (1) hand start (for smaller engines); (2) engine; (3) mounting; (4) rubber diaphragm (water seal); (5) lower unit; (6) zinc (cathodic protection); (7) boat's bottom.

but directing the thrust up or down can be used to adjust the trim of the boat for optimum running.

Saildrives bear some resemblance to outdrives, except that the engine is mounted on the bottom of the boat instead of on the transom (see Fig 8). Again, two sets of bevel gears are used to transmit the drive, but the arrangement does not provide for steering, nor for raising or lowering the propeller.

While saildrives are relatively new, outboard engines (see Fig 9) are long established and (unlike most other boat engines) are usually designed from the outset for marine use. These are discussed in chapter 9, but briefly they have good power/weight ratios and do not occupy useful space within the boat, so they are particularly suitable for small dinghies and tenders. They are also used extensively in fast runabouts, ski boats and small motor cruisers.

Whatever the choice of power unit and the method

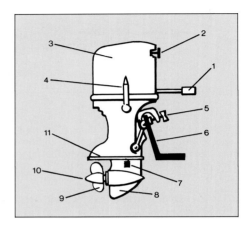

Fig 9. Outboard engine: (1) tiller arm, with twist grip throttle; (2) hand, recoil starter; (3) engine cowl; (4) gear shift; (5) screw clamps, to secure to transom; (6) transom; (7) cooling water intake; (8) skeg; (9) propeller; (10) exhaust through propeller hub; (11) cavitation plate.

of installation, a boat engine must meet certain requirements. It must develop the requisite power to propel the boat at the designed speed, with a bit in hand. It must be within the intended limits of weight, space and cost, and have a reputation for reliability. Spares and any special maintenance facilities must be available in the locality. If the engine is sufficiently small for hand starting, proper provision should be made for this. Access must be good to all necessary parts for maintenance. The generating capacity must be sufficient for the boat's electrical services. Installation must minimise noise and vibration, and engine controls must be precise and positive.

2. BASIC CONSTRUCTION

Parts of an engine – The four-stroke cycle – Two-stroke engines –
Cylinder heads – Compression ratios – Inside the block – Crankshafts –
Cylinder configurations

A marine engine converts heat produced by burning fuel into mechanical energy to turn a propeller shaft. The fuel is mixed with air, and burnt in closed cylinders inside the engine – hence the term 'internal combustion'. Either petrol or diesel fuel may be used, and the form of engine in each case has basic similarities although there are important differences in the fuel systems.

Inside each cylinder is a moving piston, which is a close fit. When the fuel/air mixture is burnt it expands, and the resulting pressure on the top (crown) of the piston drives it down on its power stroke. The pistons are linked by connecting rods to the crankshaft, so that their up-and-down motion is transformed into rotary motion of the crankshaft which in turn transmits the power to the gearbox and then to the propeller shaft.

For every pound of fuel that is burnt in the cylinder, about fifteen pounds of air are needed to give efficient combustion. In order to get this air into the combustion chamber at the top of the cylinder, and in order to remove the exhaust gases after they have been burnt, inlet valves and exhaust valves are fitted in the cylinder head at the top of the cylinder.

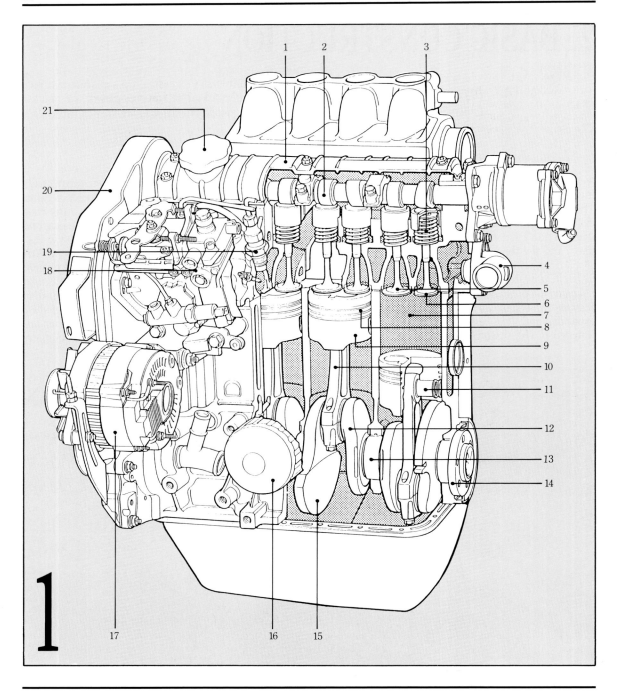

1

Fig 1. A modern four-cylinder OHC diesel engine. Basic components: (1) rocker cover; (2) camshaft; (3) valve spring; (4) cooling water outlet; (5) inlet valve; (6) exhaust valve; (7) cylinder; (8) piston rings; (9) piston; (10) connecting rod; (11) gudgeon pin; (12) crank; (13) main bearing; (14) flywheel coupling; (15) balance weight (web extension); (16) oil filter; (17) alternator; (18) fuel injection pump; (19) injector; (20) camshaft drive gear (under cover); (21) oil filler.

Fig 2. Four-stroke cycle of a petrol engine. (A) Induction. Inlet valve open and exhaust valve closed, as piston descends. Fuel and air drawn into cylinder until near bottom of stroke when inlet valve closes.
(B) Compression. Both valves closed as piston rises, compressing and heating charge.
(C) Power stroke. Near top of compression stroke, charge is ignited by spark plug. Burning gases drive piston down. Both valves closed, but near bottom of power stroke exhaust valve opens.
(D) Exhaust stroke. Exhaust valve open and inlet valve closed. Rising piston expels the burnt gases. Near top of stroke, inlet valve opens and exhaust valve closes. Cycle is then repeated.

These valves are operated by a camshaft, driven off the engine crankshaft, so that they open and close at precise moments in the cycle of operations. Fig 1 shows the basic construction of an internal combustion engine, in this case a modern four-cylinder OHC diesel engine. The features shown are similar for both petrol and diesel engines.

THE FOUR-STROKE CYCLE

Most engines work on what is called the four-stroke cycle, which means that an individual piston generates one power stroke (as described above) for every four strokes (two in each direction, making two complete revolutions of the crankshaft). This is illustrated for a petrol engine in Fig 2. On the induction stroke the inlet valve is open so that as the piston descends a mixture of fuel and air can be drawn into the cylinder. Near the bottom of the stroke the inlet valve is closed, so that on the compression stroke the piston rises and compresses the fuel/air mixture. Near the top of the compression stroke the fuel is ignited by an electric spark from

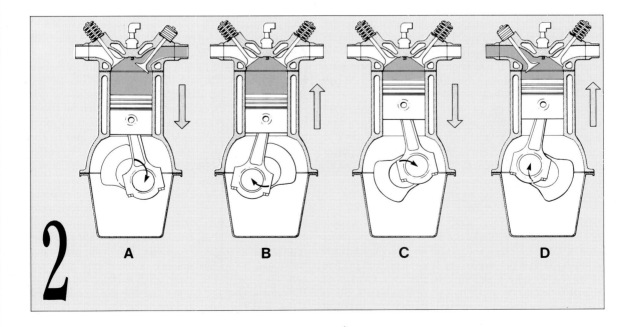

2

A   B   C   D the spark plug. On the power stroke the burning gases expand and drive the piston down, doing useful work. The exhaust valve then opens so that on the exhaust stroke the burnt gases are expelled from the cylinder. Then the exhaust valve closes and the cycle is repeated.

At this point it is necessary to explain the essential difference between petrol and diesel engines. In a petrol engine fuel is drawn into the cylinder together with air, the correct mixture being achieved by the carburettor mounted on the air inlet manifold on the side of the engine. The carburettor is designed to give different mixture strengths for different operating conditions (rich for starting and acceleration, for example, and weak for economical cruising). The fuel/air mixture is then ignited at the correct moment by the spark plug.

In a diesel engine matters are arranged slightly differently. Only air enters the cylinder on the induction stroke, and on the following compression stroke it is compressed to a higher pressure and reaches a higher temperature than the petrol/air mixture in a petrol engine. A pressure of 700lb/in^2 (49kg/cm^2) and a temperature of 1450°F (790°C) can be achieved. Just before the top of the compression stroke a fine spray of diesel fuel is injected into the top of the cylinder at a very high pressure, and this is ignited by the hot air, so that it burns and pushes the piston downwards. Diesel engines are sometimes called compression ignition engines, because they do not need an external electrical ignition system.

Since diesel engines work at higher pressures they need to be more robust in construction, and are therefore heavier than petrol units of similar power. The relative advantages and disadvantages of the two types will be discussed later.

TWO-STROKE ENGINES

Some petrol engines, and a few diesel engines, operate on a two-stroke cycle, where the various operations of getting the fuel and air into the cylinder, burning it and getting rid of the exhaust gases are arranged to take place within only two strokes of the piston (one revolution of the crank shaft). Such engines are simpler in design, have fewer moving

parts and, since each cylinder has a power stroke twice as often as with a four-stroke engine, they have good power/weight ratios. The disadvantage is that they are not so efficient – that is to say they burn more fuel for a given power output. The most obvious application of two-stroke engines is in the great majority of outboard motors, with powers ranging from 2 to 200hp (1.5 to 149kW) or more.

Both petrol and diesel engines have various features in common, which it is convenient to discuss at this point.

As shown in Fig 1, the main structural components are the cylinder head and the cylinder block. The latter is the largest single entity and usually incorporates the crankcase, which carries and surrounds the crankshaft and which is enclosed at the bottom by the sump – a reservoir for lubricating oil.

CYLINDER HEADS

The cylinder head is normally cast iron, and carries the inlet and exhaust valves for the different cylinders, the rocker gear for opening the valves, and valve springs to hold them shut. It incorporates the inlet and exhaust ports, channels for cooling water to pass through, and below it is the combustion chamber for each cylinder.

The underside of the head is machined flat to mate with the flat top of the cylinder block, the joint between them being sealed by a gasket which is usually copper/asbestos. The head is held down by nuts on a number of studs, and these nuts must be tightened in a pre-determined order and to the correct torque (tightness). A few multi-cylinder engines have separate heads for individual cylinders, or for groups of two or more cylinders.

The cylinder head and block on many engines have vertical holes through which push rods pass to operate the valve gear. Note that in a four-stroke engine the camshaft rotates at half the speed of the crankshaft. Each cam in turn lifts a tappet and a push rod, which pivots the corresponding rocker arm and opens the valve until further rotation of the cam allows the tappet and the push rod to descend, and the valve is closed by the valve spring.

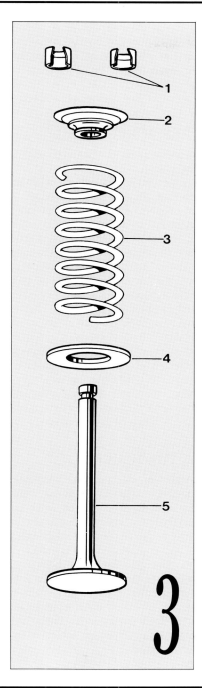

Fig 3. Valve assembly: (1) collets; (2) valve spring cap; (3) valve spring; (4) valve spring seat; (5) valve.

Some engines have two springs per valve. It is important that the correct 'tappet clearance' or 'valve tip clearance' (between the top of the valve stem and the rocker arm) is maintained because this influences the valve timing – the moments (relative to crankshaft angle) when the valve opens and shuts. This clearance is adjusted by a screw with a lock nut at the other end of the rocker arm, at the top of the push rod, using a feeler gauge to obtain the correct clearance. This clearance is normally specified with the engine cold, and is typically 0.012in (0.30mm).

Contrary to what might be expected the valves do not open and close when the piston is at the top and bottom of its stroke. The inlet valve opens just before top dead centre (TDC) and closes just after bottom dead centre (BDC). The exhaust valve opens just before BDC and closes just after TDC. Thus near TDC both valves are open together, and are said to overlap.

The positions of the cams on the camshaft (and of course the throws of the cranks on the crankshaft) dictate the firing order of the cylinders. This is either 1 3 4 2 or 1 2 4 3 for a four-cylinder engine, and typically 1 5 3 6 2 4 or 1 4 2 6 3 5 for a six-cylinder.

Valve tip clearance must be set when the valve is fully closed and the tappet is 'off the cam' – that is to say when the cam is 180° from the point of maximum lift of the tappet. This is best achieved when the valve is closed at TDC on the top of the compression stroke. In order to turn the engine over more easily remove the spark plugs from a petrol engine, or slacken the injectors of a diesel, and always turn by hand in the normal direction of rotation. Watch the inlet valve push rod as it descends. When it is fully lowered, the piston is just past BDC. Turn the engine barely another half revolution and the piston will be close to TDC on compression, allowing both the inlet and exhaust valve of that cylinder to be checked and adjusted as necessary. It helps to know the firing order of the engine, but with a little practice it is not too difficult to watch the rocker arms while slowly rotating the engine, to determine where in the cycle each piston is, and hence the position of the cam for each push rod in turn.

On top of the cylinder head is a cover which is made, like the engine sump, in a lighter material since its function is only to exclude dirt and retain the lubricating oil which is fed to the rocker gear from the engine's oil system, as described in chapter 5. The engine oil filler is usually to be found on the top of the cover. For access to the valve gear, the cylinder head cover must be removed. As applies with any other item of an engine, first clean the surrounding area very thoroughly so that no dirt can get dislodged and into the engine. There will be some form of gasket between the cover and the head, and if reasonable care is taken this should be reuseable.

Valves are held in place by two split collets which lock into a slot near the top of the valve stem. The collets bear against a dished metal washer (valve spring cap) which sits on top of the valve spring. In order to remove or replace valve springs it is necessary to use a valve spring compressor so that the collets can be released. An exploded view of a valve assembly is shown in **Fig 3**.

Any work on the valves themselves requires removal of the cylinder head. Prolonged running of an engine (particularly at light loads when it is overcooled and does not reach its optimum running temperature) will eventually lead to carbon forming in the cylinders – for example causing valves to stick in the guides – and result in loss of power, poor compression, difficult starting and smoky exhaust. Then the time has come for a top overhaul and 'decoke' – removal of the carbon deposits. This work can be undertaken by any competent amateur mechanic, given the correct tools and a good instruction book. The opportunity should be taken to grind in the valves on their seats, and then make a careful examination of valves and springs for any defects, and renew them as necessary.

Before leaving the subject of cylinder heads, it should be mentioned that so far as diesel engines are concerned there are two basic types – direct injection and indirect injection. As the name implies, with direct injection the fuel is injected straight into the top of the cylinder, with the combustion chamber usually being formed by a hollow in the crown of the piston. With indirect injection the fuel is sprayed into a small separate combustion chamber connected to the top of the cylinder by a narrow passage. For further details see chapter 4.

COMPRESSION RATIOS

The compression ratio of an engine is the volume above the piston with the piston at the top of its stroke, compared to the volume with the piston at the bottom of the stroke. In principle, the higher the compression ratio the more power the engine will deliver, but there are practical limitations.

Petrol engines have compression ratios of about 9:1. When the petrol/air mixture is ignited by the spark it should burn rapidly but smoothly, and not explode. If the compression ratio is too high, some of the mixture does in fact detonate – causing what is known as knocking or pinking. Higher compression ratios require petrol with a high octane number, i.e. four-star.

Diesel engines need higher compression ratios in order that the compressed air will reach a sufficient temperature to ignite the fuel when it is injected. With direct injection engines a typical figure is 16:1. Indirect injection engines may have higher compression ratios of 20:1 or more.

INSIDE THE BLOCK

The cylinder block and the crankcase form the largest single entity of an engine, containing the cylinders in which the pistons work and carrying the crankshaft to which are attached the piston connecting rods. The block and crankcase need to be solid and robust and are normally made from cast iron. The cylinder block also usually carries the camshaft for controlling the valves. But in some engines – like the one in Fig 1 – the camshaft is mounted on top of the cylinder head (overhead camshaft). Both the cylinder block and the head have water passages, through which water is pumped to cool the engine.

The pistons normally work in sleeves or liners of

cast iron inserted into the bores. These liners are renewable, and may be either 'wet' (where the outside of the liner is in contact with the cooling water) or 'dry' where the liner is surrounded by the metal of the cylinder block. Wet liners are much easier to replace when it comes to a major overhaul, but this is not a very likely occurence with the engine or engines of the average pleasure craft due to their limited number of running hours.

So far as the cylinder block is concerned, the most likely cause of damage is due to frost in winter – when it is important to drain out the whole system. The other matter which demands attention is the joint between the cylinder head and the cylinder block.

The pistons are arguably the most important and vulnerable part of the engine's assembly. Powered

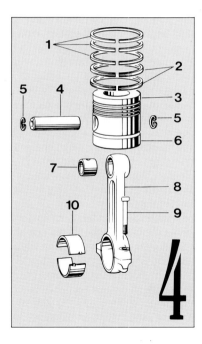

Fig 4. Piston and connecting rod assembly: (1) compression rings; (2) oil control rings; (3) piston; (4) gudgeon pin; (5) circlips; (6) piston skirt; (7) small end bearing; (8) connecting rod; (9) bolt; (10) big end bearing.

by the burning fuel, they are the driving force, converting heat into rotation. At the same time they are moving up and down very rapidly inside the cylinder. Even at the modest speed of 2000rpm a piston is reversing its direction 66 times per second. A piston therefore needs to be strong but light, and is normally made of an aluminium alloy. Piston rings, made of cast iron or cast steel, are fitted in grooves round the side of the piston near the crown to seal the gap between the piston and the cylinder. Below them a scraper ring is fitted to remove excess oil from the wall of the cylinder, and return it to the sump.

The pressure in the cylinder may exceed $1000lb/in^2$ ($70kg/cm^2$) so it is important to maintain a good gas seal, and the fit of the rings in their grooves and in the cylinder is vital for good performance. Wear will result in loss of power, poor starting, exhaust smoke, high oil consumption and uneven running.

Each piston is secured to the top end of its connecting rod by a gudgeon pin, or wrist pin, about which the small end of the connecting rod can pivot, moving up and down with the piston (see **Fig 4**). The gudgeon pin is located in the piston body by circlips (spring clips) at each end. The big end (lower end) of the connecting rod is bolted round one of the crankpins of the crankshaft. Connecting rods have an 'H' section and are normally made from a steel forging or stamping.

CRANKSHAFTS

The details and design of crankshafts vary with different engines and the number of cylinders, but basically the crankshaft has journals (accurately machined cylindrical portions) which rotate in the main bearings of the engine, and webs or cranks which join the journals to the crankpins – on which the big end bearings of the connecting rods rotate. A four-cylinder engine has four cranks (see Fig 5) each with its connecting rod and piston, and ideally five main bearings – one each end and one between each pair of cranks. The latter are shaped to improve the balance of the whole assembly. At its rear end the crankshaft is attached to a flywheel, which promotes smoother running. As is discussed in more detail

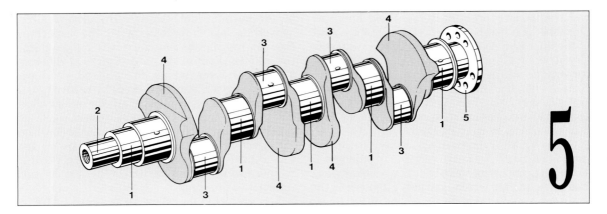

Fig 5. Crankshaft: (1) crankshaft journals which rotate in main bearings; (2) front end, fitting for pulley for vibration damper; (3) crankpin which carries big end of connecting rod; (4) balance weight (web extension); (5) flange for connection to flywheel.

when dealing with lubrication in chapter 5, oil is fed under pressure to the main bearings, and from there through oilways in the crankshaft to the big end bearings, and then in turn through oilways in the connecting rods of larger engines to lubricate the small end bearings. With small engines these are often lubricated by splash and oil mist from the big end bearings in order not to weaken the connecting rod with a drilled hole.

Most crankshafts are forged from special steel, with the main and big end journals hardened. Both the main and big end bearings are replaceable. In the event of untoward damage to crankshaft journals it is possible for the crankshaft to be reground and for undersize bearings to be fitted.

CYLINDER CONFIGURATIONS

An engine with just one cylinder and piston can only generate a certain power, produces an uneven torque, and suffers from large out of balance forces. The uneven torque can be overcome to some extent by fitting a large flywheel, but there is no practical way of eliminating the vibration caused by the reciprocating action of a single piston. Consequently,

although there are some small single-cylinder marine engines, the great majority are multi-cylinder units. The arrangement of the cylinders can vary.

Even the addition of one more cylinder gives much better balance and smoother running. Two cylinders may be arranged with them vertical and in-line, or sometimes with the cylinders horizontal on either side of the crankshaft – called horizontally opposed. This latter arrangement gives a shorter crankshaft and improved balance because the movement of one piston is offset by the movement of the other in the opposite direction.

The majority of marine engines generating powers of between 30 and 80hp (22 and 60kW) have four cylinders in-line. Above this power six cylinders in-line are the most common, giving better balance than four-cylinder units.

V engines, with the cylinders arranged in V-shaped pairs, are most popular for the larger petrol outdrives, but there are several V-configuration diesels. The V arrangement does produce a squat and compact engine, but V4 engines have inherent vibration problems and the V6 is not so good in this respect as a six-cylinder in-line engine. V8 engines, with an angle of 90°, are extremely well balanced and smooth running.

It should be mentioned that, in order to facilitate installation where there is limited height in the machinery compartment, some in-line engines are arranged with the cylinders inclined to the vertical, and even in some cases horizontal.

3. PETROL (GASOLENE) ENGINES

Petrol systems – Fixed-jet carburettors – Variable-jet carburettors –
Ignition systems – Spark plugs – Safety first

Petrol engines are now far less common than diesels, except in two particular applications where they really come into their own. One is with outboard motors, almost entirely powered by two-stroke petrol units which are discussed in more detail in chapter 9, and the other is with outdrives, the majority of which have four-stroke petrol units. There are of course other inboard installations powered by four-stroke petrol engines, and nearly all such engines are marinised versions of automotive units which will largely be familiar to anyone who takes an interest in what goes on under the bonnet of their car.

With most four-stroke petrol engines fuel is drawn into the cylinder together with the air on the (downward) induction stroke of the piston. In a few modern petrol engines the fuel is injected into the cylinder in a manner similar to a diesel engine. But for our purposes we can forget such innovations, and consider the function of the carburettor which normally provides the correct air/petrol mixture for different running conditions. Although what follows is directed mainly at four-stroke petrol engines, many of the general principles regarding carburation and ignition apply equally to two-stroke engines.

PETROL SYSTEMS

The carburettor's function is to supply the engine with the proper mixture of vaporised fuel and air over the full range of operating conditions. A mixture of about fifteen parts of air to one part of petrol (by weight) is needed to give good combustion under average running conditions but, for example, a much richer mixture (more petrol) is required when starting from cold and a slightly weaker mixture (less petrol) for economical cruising. A richer mixture than normal is needed for slow running, for accelerating, and at higher powers. To cope with these demands, carburettors tend to be complicated, and therefore delicate, parts with which an owner is not encouraged to tamper. However, it is still useful to have an idea of how they function and what to look for if things go wrong. An engine's instruction manual should give information about the type of carburettor fitted, and what adjustments are within the capacity of the average owner.

Before going any further, remember that petrol can be dangerous. The vapour is heavier than air, and very explosive. When working on any petrol system always mop up any spills or leaks promptly, and keep the space well ventilated. No naked lights or sparks (which can all too easily be generated when operating or testing electrical systems) must be allowed in the vicinity.

The carburettor needs supplies of fuel and air, and to avoid problems both must be clean. So far as fuel is concerned cleanliness starts with the tank – and what is put in it. If the contents of the fuel tank can be kept clean and free of water (which may appear from condensation on the walls of the tank), many of the problems that can occur with marine engines will be eliminated. Although it may slow down the rate of fuelling, it is worth considering a large filling funnel that incorporates a fine gauze filter. In the days when boat engines were replenished from cans, it was not unknown for people to filter their petrol through chamois leather. That might be considered a bit too laborious now, but any steps that can be taken to eliminate dirt will be well rewarded. To prevent, or at least minimise, condensation it is best to fill up when you return to a harbour, rather than leave a tank half full. However, it is best not to store petrol over the winter months since it does not improve with age.

Petrol tanks should be made of lead-coated steel, copper (tinned on the inside), brass or galvanised steel, and should be well baffled. There should be a large access plate for cleaning and, if possible, a sump and drain cock for drawing off samples. The deck filler point must be well labelled (people have been known to put fresh water down the wrong hole) and fitted with a good watertight cap which must be replaced immediately fuelling is completed. If a flexible filling pipe is fitted, the filling point and the tank must be electrically bonded. The fuel tank vent must be led to a protected position outboard of the hull, and be fitted with a flame arrestor. A typical petrol system is shown in Fig 1.

Petrol pipes should be of seamless copper, copper-nickel or stainless steel, with the final length to the engine made of an approved flexible tubing. There should be a minimum of joints, and piping should be securely clipped in position. At the point where

the pipe comes out of the tank, there must be a shut-off valve, easily accessible for operation and with an extension spindle for remote control. In some boats solenoid-operated valves are fitted, which switch on and off with the ignition system.

Petrol is pumped from the tank to the carburettor by a lift pump, mounted on the engine. Between the pump and the tank, in a position where it is easily accessible for examination and cleaning, there should be a pre-filter, the first line of defence against any moisture or dirt. Quite sensibly these filters often have glass bowls, so that there is visual evidence of any contamination, but these are forbidden by certain navigational authorities because they are considered dangerous. Additional filters are usually fitted in the lift pump and at the inlet to the carburettor.

An internal combustion engine uses a great deal of air. We have already noted that to burn one pound of fuel requires about fifteen pounds of air, and at normal atmospheric pressure and temperature fifteen pounds of air occupy nearly 200 cubic feet — about the size of a small cabin. From the point of view of cylinder wear, air filtration is important,

Fig 1. A diagrammatic layout of a petrol system: (1) petrol tank; (2) internal baffle; (3) sump and drain cock; (4) air escape; (5) filling pipe from deck; (6) remotely controlled shut-off valve; (7) solenoid-operated shut-off valve; (8) pre-filter/water separator; (9) fuel lift pump; (10) carburettor; (11) air filter, incorporating flame trap; (12) inlet manifold; (13) exhaust manifold; (14) exhaust pipe; (15) propeller shaft; (16) exhaust fan sucking from bilge; (17) air inlet; (18) throttle control.

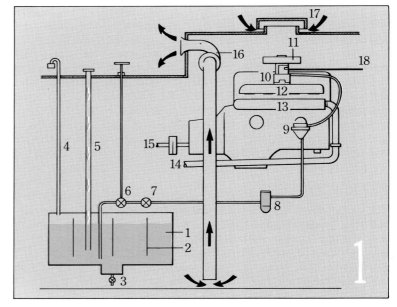

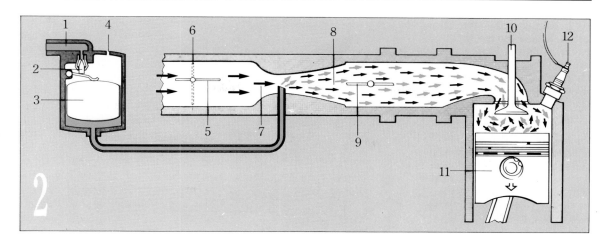

Fig 2. Basic principles of the carburettor: (1) petrol supply from fuel lift pump; (2) float-controlled needle valve, to maintain level in float chamber; (3) float; (4) air vent; (5) choke (strangler) in open position; (6) choke closed; (7) air flowing into venturi speeds up, and pressure drops, thereby sucking petrol from float chamber; (8) petrol mixes with air; (9) throttle (shown open) controlling the flow of petrol/air mixture to cylinder; (10) inlet valve; (11) piston descending on induction stroke; (12) spark plug.

although obviously less so in the open sea than in coastal or inland waters. The filter unit has other functions – it silences the noise of the air intake, it is designed to damp out pressure fluctuations in the inlet manifold, and it includes a flame trap to prevent a backfire igniting any petrol vapour outside the engine. It has to perform these tasks, but at the same time it must not restrict the air flow into the carburettor too much. There are two main types of air filter – one with a replaceable paper element, and one with a wire mesh filter which may incorporate an oil bath. Every season the filter needs to be examined and cleaned, and any paper element replaced. When replacing the filter make sure that if fits squarely on the inlet flange and that the joint is good. Most air filters incorporate some form of crankcase breather for gases that get past the pistons and into the crankcase.

The basic principles on which a carburettor works are shown in Fig 2. As the piston descends, the filtered air is drawn into a restriction, called the venturi, which increases the air speed and causes a drop in pressure. This partial vacuum sucks petrol from the float chamber, where it is maintained at a certain level by a float-controlled needle valve. The petrol mixes with the air and passes through the inlet manifold into the cylinder. The throttle, on the downstream side of the venturi, controls the flow of the petrol/air mixture and hence the power of the engine. The choke, upstream of the venturi, increases the mixture strength for cold starting and may be controlled manually or perhaps by an automatic device which keeps it closed until the engine starts to warm up.

FIXED-JET CARBURETTORS

Carburettors fall into two main types. The most common are the fixed-jet (or constant-choke) type where the orifice areas are constant and the depression alters. Air flow and petrol flow do not vary in the same way with change of depression – as the flow of air through the venturi speeds up and its pressure drops, so the air becomes lighter and the mixture would become progressively richer. Compensating arrangements are therefore needed in order to keep the petrol/air mixture at the required level throughout the range of engine speed.

Fig 3. Fixed-jet carburettor: (1) air inlet; (2) choke flap (open); (3) venturi; (4) needle valve, controlling level in float chamber; (5) air vent; (6) main jet; (7) emulsifying tube; (8) air correction jet; (9) idling jet; (10) idling adjustment; (11) throttle (shown almost open); (12) accelerator pump, connected to throttle linkage. The solid colour indicates petrol flow into the venturi at nearly full power. The coloured dotted chain shows how extra fuel is delivered into the venturi by the accelerator pump. At idling speeds, with throttle almost closed, the level in the main emulsion well drops, a partial vacuum is caused in the inlet manifold and fuel is then drawn via the idling jet as shown by the coloured dots.

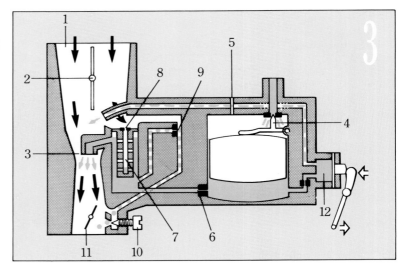

In a fixed-jet carburettor (see Fig 3) this may be achieved by mixing some air with the fuel in an emulsion tube or correction jet consisting of two concentric tubes into which petrol is drawn before being discharged into the air stream where it flows through the venturi. The inner tube is connected to the air supply upstream of the venturi, and as engine speed increases so more air enters it through an air correction jet. The inner tube has a number of holes drilled in it at different levels, and as engine speed rises the petrol level within the inner tube is depressed thereby exposing more holes to the air above and weakening the mixture.

Another way of achieving the same result is with a compensating jet whereby with increasing engine speed more air is supplied as the fuel level drops in a well alongside the float chamber, in order to weaken the mixture and thus compensate for the richer mixture from the main jet – which is designed to provide a relatively weak mixture for economical cruising.

For higher powers an additional jet comes into play to give a slightly richer mixture, while for sudden acceleration there is a separate accelerator pump, connected to the throttle mechanism, which discharges extra fuel into the air flow just upstream

of the venturi. For satisfactory idling, an additional idling jet is needed so that with the throttle almost closed petrol and air are provided through a separate circuit which has its own mixture adjustment.

From this brief description of fixed-jet carburettors it should be evident that they have a large number of small passages, jets and discharge holes – any of which are liable to blockage should any dirt be in the fuel. On the other hand they have no moving parts, so they are not susceptible to wear or to damage, except such as may be inflicted by careless cleaning or dismantling.

Any dirt that gets past the filtering arrangements (perhaps if the fuel tank has been allowed to empty) is liable to accumulate in the float chamber, so it is a good idea to examine and clean this from time to time. First have a thorough clean-up all round that area, otherwise you may only succeed in putting in more dirt than you get out. This applies to any dismantling of an engine. The securing bolts may be of different lengths, so note their positions for replacement. Take care when removing any joint which will need to be replaced. Check the operation of the needle valve and make sure that the float controlling it is not punctured. Use a piece of lint-free rag, soaked in petrol, to clean out the float chamber. If it is necessary to clean a jet, remove it carefully while noting the setting. Jets should be cleaned with an air blast – never with a piece of wire which will damage the orifice. On reassembly make sure that surfaces are clean, joints are correctly placed, and that all connections are properly tightened – remember that petrol leaks are potentially lethal.

VARIABLE-JET CARBURETTORS

Before leaving carburettors, mention must be made of the variable-jet or constant-depression type, of which SU and Stromberg carburettors are examples. Here the area of the venturi can be varied in order

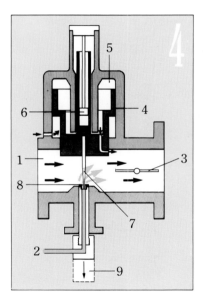

Fig 4. Variable-jet carburettor, shown at full throttle when the piston rises to enlarge the area of the venturi and also increase the flow of petrol. At lower throttle settings the piston falls as indicated by the two arrows, reducing both air and petrol flows. (1) Air inlet; (2) from float chamber; (3) throttle (open); (4) piston (raised); (5) suction chamber; (6) damper, to slow rise of piston; (7) tapered needle valve; (8) jet; (9) choke control lowers jet assembly as shown, dotted, to increase mixture strength.

to maintain a steady vacuum at the single jet. An illustration of the SU carburettor is shown in Fig 4.

The area of the venturi is controlled by a piston which moves vertically inside a suction chamber its position being regulated by the throttle opening. At low engine speeds, when there is little air flow, the piston falls and restricts the venturi. As the throttle is opened and the air speed increases, so the partial vacuum above the piston increases and the piston rises to enlarge the venturi and give more air flow.

Attached to the bottom of the piston is a tapered needle valve, which controls the flow of fuel. As the piston rises so does the needle, to allow more petrol to flow from the jets into the airstream. The relative positions and shapes of the jet and the needle valve maintain the correct mixture strength. A damper is fitted above the piston to slow down its rise when the throttle is opened. This increases the partial vacuum at the jet so that extra fuel is drawn out to provide a temporarily richer mixture. It is important that this damper is kept topped up with engine oil, or acceleration will suffer. To help start the engine from cold, the choke control lowers the jet assembly, which enlarges the area for the fuel to escape at the jet and therefore gives a richer mixture.

IGNITION SYSTEMS

Having got the right mixture of petrol and air into the cylinder, the next problem is to burn it at the right moment. This is done by the ignition system, which momentarily passes a very high voltage across the points of a spark plug. Until recently it would have been corrected to say that this was achieved either by a magneto or by a coil, which gives a better spark at starting speeds. However, electronic capacitor discharge (CD) ignition systems are now used on virtually all new petrol engines (whether four-stroke inboards or two-stroke outboards).

Many magneto and coil-type systems are already in existence, however, and we cannot overlook them. They both work on the principle that when an electric current flows in a coil of wire it produces a magnetic field, and that conversely if a magnetic field breaks down a current will be generated in a coil of wire within that field. In practice two windings surround a soft iron core, to concentrate the magnetic field. When the current in the low voltage primary winding (which has relatively few turns of wire) is broken, a very high voltage is induced in the secondary winding (which has a very large number of turns of wire). This high tension (HT) current is passed via a distributor to the selected spark plug – the process being repeated to each in turn. Where some 30,000 volts are involved, in the HT circuit, it is obvious that the insulation arrangements need to be first class. Fig 5 shows a diagram of a typical coil ignition system. The moment that the spark is created is determined by the contact breaker, operated by a cam on the distributor shaft which rotates at half crankshaft speed. The number of lobes on the cam corresponds to the number of cylinders. A condenser is fitted across the contact breaker points to suppress arcing when they open and to intensify the voltage

in the secondary winding. Another refinement is the provision of automatic ignition advance for higher engine speeds, which is likely to be achieved by a centrifugal mechanism on the distributor shaft supplemented by a vacuum advance operated from the inlet manifold.

Since the distributor and its contact breaker (together with the sparking plugs) are the parts of the ignition system that lend themselves to owner maintenance they deserve closer attention. At least once a season remove the distributor cap (normally held by two spring clips) and inspect it internally for dirt or cracks, either of which would allow the HT voltage to run to earth. Check all the terminals together with the carbon brush which is in the centre of the cap and bears on the rotor arm. Clean the inside of the cap with a lint-free rag moistened with petrol.

Check that the plastic heel of the cam follower is

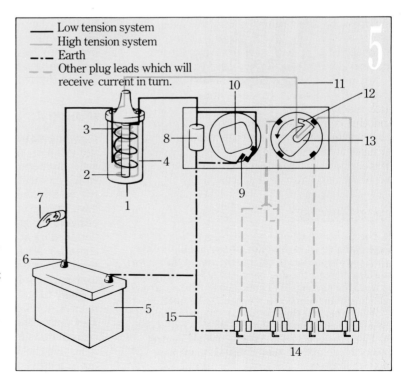

Fig 5. Coil ignition system: (1) ignition coil; (2) soft iron core; (3) primary (LT) winding; (4) secondary (HT) winding; (5) battery; (6) battery terminal; (7) ignition switch; (8) condenser; (9) contact breaker, operated by cams on distributor drive; (10) cams; (11) HT lead; (12) distributor; (13) rotating distributor arm, directs current to each plug in turn; (14) spark plugs; (15) earth return to battery.

in good condition, since this can wear or even break. Lightly grease the faces of the cam. Put a few drops of light oil on the centrifugal timing advance, on the pivot point of the moving contact, and (if fitted) on the felt pad at the top of the distributor shaft under the rotor arm.

Turn the engine over slowly by hand until the contact breaker points are fully open, and examine them carefully for any sign of pitting, in which case they should be replaced. As a temporary measure they can be dressed up with a very small file. In any case the gap must be checked with a feeler gauge against the clearance given in the engine handbook, which is likely to be about 0.015in (0.35mm). It is important that the contacts are correctly located so that the two faces are square to each other and completely opposite.

Any significant variation from the correct gap clearance will affect ignition timing, but otherwise there is no reason for the timing to change unless parts of the engine are dismantled for some reason. If necessary the timing can be checked against marks inscribed on the flywheel, but the best way to check the performance of an engine is with modern electronic test equipment (see chapter 11).

Not much needs to be said about capacitor discharge (CD) ignition systems, since they eliminate such mechanical features as contact breaker points and the conventional rotor arm. They are more resistant to sea water and they also deliver higher voltages to help starting and to keep plugs in better shape. However, they do not lend themselves to maintenance by amateur mechanics.

SPARK PLUGS

To the uninitiated, one spark plug looks much like another but they have important differences. Fig 6 shows a typical plug: the HT current passes down the central electrode and then jumps the gap between that and the earth or side electrode. Some plugs have a longer or shorter reach – that is to say the threaded portion is longer or shorter depending on the design of the cylinder head. Plugs are also described as 'hot' or 'cold' depending on their ability to transfer heat away from the end of the central

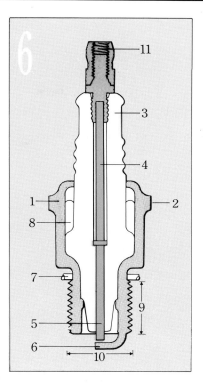

Fig 6. Spark plug: (1) plug body; (2) hexagon to take plug spanner; (3) ceramic insulator; (4) arrow shows direction of current flow; (5) central electrode; (6) side (or earth) electrode; (7) sealing washer; (8) sealing gasket; (9) reach of plug; (10) diameter of thread; (11) terminal screw.

electrode and into the cylinder head. This is determined by how far down the insulator enclosing the central electrode is in contact with the inside of the threaded portion of the plug body, and hence the distance that the heat has to travel to escape. A cold plug, which transfers heat quickly, is used in high-performance engines to prevent overheating and pre-ignition. A hot plug runs at a higher temperature in a cooler running engine in order to burn off any deposits from combustion that would otherwise form. Use only the designated type of plug, the choice of which also depends on the compression ratio, speed range and mixture strength of the engine.

To give a good spark the plug gap needs to be fairly wide (as specified in the engine handbook, and usually about 0.030in or 0.80mm). This needs to be checked regularly since the electrodes get eroded and also need cleaning. When removing spark plugs first make sure that the plug leads are numbered so that they can be replaced correctly. Then clean the area round each plug, and always use a proper plug spanner. Make quite sure that nothing (such as a screwed terminal from the top of a plug) can fall into the cylinder by placing a piece of rag over the opening.

The business end of the plug should be washed in white spirit or petrol and thoroughly cleaned with sandpaper (not emery paper). Make sure that the surfaces of the electrodes are flat, using a thin and smooth file if necessary and taking care to wash away any filings. Adjust the gap by gently bending the side electrode – do not put any pressure on the central electrode – and using a feeler gauge to measure the clearance. Cleaning and adjusting a set of plugs properly takes a certain amount of time, and it is advisable to carry a spare set on board so that in the event of trouble they can be substituted quickly. When replacing plugs do not overtighten them. Ideally a torque spanner should be used, but otherwise put them in hand tight and then tighten them not more than half a turn with the spanner.

The appearance of a spark plug when it is removed is a good indication of the health of an engine, and notes on this together with general comments on troubleshooting with petrol engines are given in chapter 12.

SAFETY FIRST

Although the fuel is potentially dangerous, a petrol engine which is properly installed, well maintained and sensibly used can be perfectly safe. But any escape of petrol is a serious matter, so it is important to have a regular check of all joints in the system. Installation has already been mentioned, and any petrol-engined boat should have a properly fitted (spark-free) exhaust fan which sucks from the bottom of the engine space. This should always be run for at least five minutes before starting an engine, but in addition it is sensible to open the hatch and have a good smell around, since the human nose is a good detector of petrol fumes. There are electronic devices which will do the same job 24 hours a day – plus giving warning of high bilge levels, intruders or heat caused by a fire.

Never run an engine without the air filter flame arrestor in place. A skipper must insist on no smoking and no naked lights whenever work is being done on engines or when refuelling. Although strictly outside the subject of engines, a petrol-engined boat should certainly have a full quota of fire-fighting equipment, including a fixed installation which can be remotely controlled to cover the tank space and the engine compartment.

4. DIESEL ENGINES

Diesel fuel systems – Fuel injection pumps – Injectors – Venting the fuel system – Turbochargers

In any internal combustion engine a high compression ratio is desirable for fuel economy and maximum power output. The compression ratio of a petrol engine is limited by the characteristics of the fuel, since high temperature and pressure in the cylinder can cause spontaneous combustion ahead of the flame spreading from the sparking plug, resulting in detonation (referred to as 'knocking' or 'pinking'). In extreme cases pre-ignition can occur before the spark takes place, and since this happens before top dead centre is reached the negative work results in loss of power as well as possible damage.

Detonation and pre-ignition can be prevented by using the correct fuel, by good engine design and by the right choice of spark plug. The anti-knock properties of petrol are indicated by its octane number, which in turn is shown by the familiar 'star' rating at the pump.

Diesel engines, with their high compression ratios, are more efficient than their petrol rivals. In addition, the fuel burns more slowly, so that there is a more gradual increase in cylinder temperature and pressure, resulting in a more even torque at the crankshaft.

In general construction the four-stroke diesel, although more sturdy, is similar to a petrol engine. The main difference is that in a diesel engine the fuel is injected into the combustion chamber at very high pressure, at a controlled rate and at precisely the right moment – and is atomised into tiny particles and distributed throughout the combustion chamber.

Great attention is paid to cylinder head design, and there are two main types of combustion chamber. In many smaller high-speed engines, the fuel is injected into a precombustion chamber (see Fig 1), where it begins to burn before expanding through a narrow passage into the cylinder proper – thereby creating turbulence with the air to utilise as much oxygen as possible. This is known as indirect injection. Unfortunately, it involves a large surface area inside the combustion chambers which gives a high heat loss, reducing thermal efficiency and making

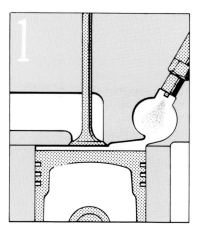

Fig 1. Indirect injection (precombustion) chamber, with pintle atomiser.

starting more difficult. High compression ratios are required to overcome this, and heating (glow) plugs are fitted in the precombustion chamber to aid starting. Direct injection is normally found in larger engines, but it is becoming more common in smaller ones. Fuel is injected straight into the top of the cylinder (see Fig 2). This gives a simple

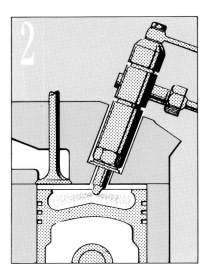

Fig 2. Direct injection (open combustion) chamber, with multi-hole atomiser. Note the hollow in the piston crown to create turbulence.

design, with a small surface area to reduce heat loss and to assist cold starting.

Fuel injection pumps and fuel injectors (atomisers) are precision parts which cannot be serviced by a boat owner. But some knowledge of their working is necessary, if only to drive home the most important fact that their moving parts have very fine clearances which must be kept scrupulously clean at all times.

DIESEL FUEL SYSTEMS

The arrangement of a typical fuel system for a four-cylinder diesel is shown in **Fig 3**. The importance of clean fuel has already been emphasised in relation to petrol engines. Diesel fuel should conform to the specification given in the engine handbook, and normally this will be BS 2869: 1967 – Class A1 and A2 in the United Kingdom, ASTM/D975 in the United States, J.O. 14/9/57 Gas Oil in France, DIN-51601 (1967) in Germany, Cuna-Gas Oil NC-630-01 (1957) in Italy and SIS.15.54.32 (1969) in Sweden.

With a diesel system there is an even greater need for thorough filtration. Before the lift pump (which delivers fuel from the tank to the injection pump) there must be a primary filter of the sedimenter type (see Fig 4), designed to separate water from the fuel as well as filtering larger solid particles. It should have a transparent bowl so that contamination is evident, and the more sophisticated types have an electronic device which sounds an alarm or shuts off the supply if the water reaches a certain level. The bowl should be inspected before going to sea, and should be drained and cleaned at regular intervals.

A secondary filter-agglomerator (see Fig 5) is fitted between the lift pump and the injection pump. This is a much finer filter which will also trap any droplets of water that are still suspended in the fuel. The filter needs to be drained off regularly.

The secondary filter element must be changed at the intervals given in the engine handbook, and more frequently if any contamination has been experienced. This is one of the few jobs on the fuel system within the scope of an amateur mechanic, and it should certainly be done at least once a year – at the start of the season perhaps.

First thoroughly clean off the area all round the filter. (As a matter of practice all external parts of an engine should be kept clean at all times, because this makes any leaks more obvious.) Drain the contents of the filter into a suitable can to take ashore. Hold the base of the filter and undo the central bolt. Twist and pull the base downwards to release it. Note how the element and the sealing rings are positioned so that the filter can be reassembled properly. Discard the old element and sealing rings. Clean the base with a lint-free cloth and wash it out with diesel fuel. Clean out and close the drain plug. With the cloth or a brush clean the underside of the filter head, including the groove for the sealing ring. Then reassemble the filter with the new element and seals, turning it so that it slides over the centre 'O' ring. Be careful not to overtighten the bolt. Before starting the engine, vent the fuel system to get rid of air that will have entered – as described below. This task will be reduced if the filter is filled with fuel before replacement. When the engine is running check the filter for leaks.

Fig 3. Diesel engine fuel system:
(1) primary filter (sedimenter); (2)
drain cock; (3) fuel lift pump; (4)
secondary filter-agglomerator; (5)
drain cock; (6) in-line fuel
injection pump; (7) mechanical
governor housing; (8) speed
control lever; (9) auto-advance
coupling; (10) cold start (excess
fuel) button; (11) engine stop; (12)
boost control unit; (13) delivery
valve holder; (14) idling damper
(anti-stall device); (15) high-
pressure fuel pipe; (16) atomiser.
The letters indicate typical venting
positions: (A) vent point at
secondary filter; (B) vent screw at
injection pump (there may be two);
(C) vent point at atomiser.

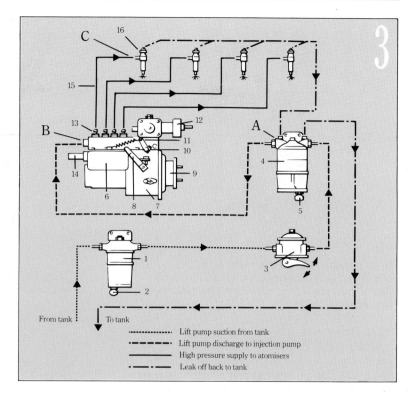

FUEL INJECTION PUMPS

Following the flow of fuel, the next component is
the fuel injection pump. This is almost certain to
be either an in-line pump with a separate pumping
plunger for each cylinder, or a distributor pump
(DPA) where there is one central pump with a rotating element which distributes the output to each
cylinder's injector in rotation. There is another form
of fuel injection, not often found in pleasure craft,
where each cylinder has its own combined pump
and injector.

It is vital that precisely the correct amount of
fuel is delivered to each cylinder in turn. With the
in-line type of pump, where a plunger for each
cylinder is mounted vertically above and operated
by a camshaft driven off the engine, this is achieved
by each plunger having a spiral groove cut into it.
The plungers have a constant length of stroke, but

by rotating them within their cylinders the effective
pumping action is varied from 'no fuel' (stop) to
maximum (full power). The plungers are rotated
together by a control rod, which is linked to the
engine governor. Above each plunger is a delivery
valve which has three functions. First it acts as a
non-return valve when the plunger is descending
on its filling (non-pumping) stroke; second it helps
a rapid build-up of pressure in the line to the
atomiser; and third it gives a quick cut-off when
the plunger finishes its effective pumping stroke.

The pump plungers are lubricated by the small
amount of fuel which leaks past the tiny clearance in
their barrels. The only maintenance needed for an in-
line pump is to drain and replenish the cam box with
engine oil after every 100 hours running. Even that is
unnecessary if the camshaft is lubricated from the
engine's pressure system.

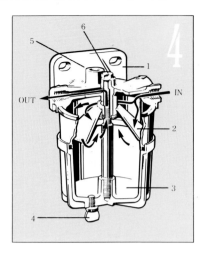

Fig 4. Primary filter (sedimenter): (1) filter head; (2) sedimenter, element or diffuser; (3) sedimenter chamber; (4) drain plug; (5) venting position; (6) central bolt.

The power of a petrol engine is controlled by the throttle – a butterfly valve in the air inlet. As this is opened more air and petrol enter the cylinders and power is increased. With a diesel engine the power is controlled by the amount of fuel delivered by the injection pump to the injectors. The pistons draw in about the same amount of air on each induction stroke, regardless of engine load or rpm. At low outputs, when very little fuel is injected, only part of the available oxygen is consumed in the combustion process. As power is increased more fuel is injected, until at full power nearly all the available oxygen is used – a small margin is preserved in the engine design to ensure complete combustion and avoid harmful emissions.

In order to achieve a steady running speed under variable load governors have to be fitted to diesel engines to control the amount of fuel delivered to the atomisers. Some mechanical governors only control the fuel supply at idling and at maximum speeds. These settings can be adjusted quite easily, but the maximum speed setting (which may in any case be sealed by the maker) should only be attempted if a reliable tachometer is available. Other types of governor

for in-line pumps may be either mechanical or pneumatic (controlled by the pressure in the air inlet manifold) and govern the engine throughout the speed range. Governors of distributor pumps (described below) are either mechanical or hydraulic in operation. In each case the governor is linked to the control of the fuel pump, which in turn is connected (usually by cable) to the throttle lever at the helmsman's position. The helmsman selects a certain throttle setting for the required rpm, and

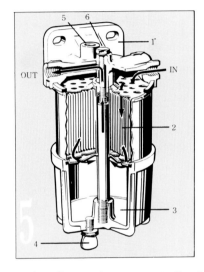

Fig 5. Secondary filter-agglomerator: (1) filter head; (2) filter-agglomerator paper element; (3) sedimenter chamber; (4) drain plug; (5) venting position; (6) central bolt.

the governor then adjusts the fuel supply accordingly. Governors seldom give trouble, but they need whatever routine maintenance is stated in the engine handbook which may include lubrication of the diaphragm in a pneumatic governor and general lubrication and cleaning. If the governor hunts at idling speed the cause may quite likely be in the engine itself, rather than the governor.

A separate stop control puts the injection pump to the 'no fuel' setting to stop the engine. In older installations this may be a simple, spring-loaded knob at the control position, but most installations have an electrically operated stop control wired into the key switch. Whenever any difficulty is experienced with starting, check that this control has returned to the 'run' position.

Modern fuel injection pumps may be fitted with an auto-advance coupling, whereby with increasing rpm the timing of the fuel injection is automatically advanced, by an amount which might be as much as 12° between idling and maximum rpm in the case of a high speed engine.

For starting the engine an excess fuel device is fitted. One reason for this is because at low cranking speeds more fuel leaks past the plungers of the fuel pump during each stroke just because there is more time for it to do so. The device may be set either automatically or manually, and the design is such as to prevent excess fuel being supplied once the engine is running.

Distributor (DPA) fuel pumps incorporate similar features to in-line pumps but the general arrangement and methods of operation are very different. There is a single pumping unit, from which the fuel is distributed to each atomiser in turn through radial passages – spaced at 90° for a four-cylinder engine and at 60° for a six-cylinder one. Because each cylinder is supplied in turn by a single pumping unit it is easier to ensure that each receives the same quantity of fuel, giving more even loading and smoother running. The supply of fuel is controlled by a metering valve at the inlet port, operated by a mechanical or hydraulic governor which may include an anti-stall device to prevent the engine stopping when it is throttled down to tickover. Distributor pumps are very compact, but they are even more susceptible to dirt or water than in-line pumps.

INJECTORS

And so we come to the last important links in the chain of fuel injection equipment – the injectors (or atomisers). In them the metered quantity of fuel delivered at very high pressure by the injection pump lifts a spring-loaded valve off its seat and emerges as an atomised spray from the nozzle tip. On completion of the injection the spring returns the valve to its seat, ready to repeat the process –

25 times per second at 3000rpm. Atomisers are secured to the cylinder head by studs or bolts, and are made of steel to withstand the high injection pressures used – in the range of 1500–3000lb/in^2 (100–200 atmospheres).

Slight leakage of fuel past the needle valve stem serves to provide lubrication, and this leakage is returned from a connection at or near the top of the injector through a leak-off pipe back to the fuel tank.

Injectors come in different forms, depending on combustion chamber design, but there are two main types. Multi-hole injectors (see Fig 6) are commonly used on direct injection engines and have two or more holes at the nozzle tip. Pintle type injectors have the end of the needle in the form of a pin

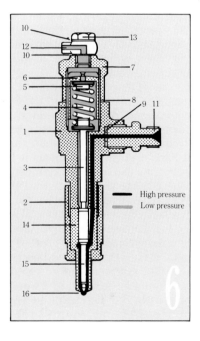

High pressure
Low pressure

Fig 6. Multi-hole atomiser: (1) nozzle holder; (2) nozzle nut; (3) spindle; (4) spring; (5) upper spring plate; (6) spring cap nut; (7) cap nut; (8) joint washer; (9) joint washer; (10) joint washer; (11) inlet adaptor; (12) leak-off connection; (13) banjo bolt; (14) nozzle; (15) needle valve; (16) spray holes.

(pintle) protruding through a hole in the lower face of the nozzle. The pin is tapered inwards so that a conical spray is emitted, the spray pattern depending on the shape of the pintle. This type of injector is used with indirect injection engines. A variation is the Pintaux, which incorporates an auxiliary spray hole to direct fuel towards the heater plug and assist cold starting. Pintle nozzles have the advantage that they tend to keep themselves cleaner than the multi-hole type. It should be obvious that only the specified injector must be used in a particular engine.

Provided that the fuel is clean, most injectors should run for a long period (typically 1000 hours) before they need servicing. However, with some high performance, turbocharged engines this service interval is very much reduced. Symptoms of injector trouble (usually caused by a build-up of carbon) include intermittent misfiring, a smoky exhaust, a pronounced knock, engine vibration, a lack of power, increased fuel consumption, and engine overheating. These symptoms may of course be the result of other engine defects.

A simple way of detecting whether or not a particular injector is at fault is to run the engine at a fast idling speed and to slacken the pipe union two or three turns at each injector in succession. Take care not to discharge fuel everywhere, and do not place your hand over the spray since the high pressure can penetrate the skin. The cylinder at fault is the one where there is no change in the engine beat or speed. The misfiring may be due to factors other than a faulty injector, such as a sticky delivery valve in the fuel pump or a defective valve or piston ring, so for a more comprehensive test on the actual injector, move it from the suspect cylinder to another one and see if the symptoms are repeated.

Injectors should be serviced in a workshop that is equipped with the necessary tools, cleaning equipment and test pump. For this reason a boat should always carry a spare set of injectors, together with their associated high-pressure fuel pipes, so that in the event of trouble a spare can easily be fitted.

Before removing an injector, clean the surrounding area carefully. Undo the union nuts at each end of the high-pressure fuel pipe – at the pump and at the atomiser – and remove it. Immediately cap each end of the pipe and the fuel pump orifice to prevent dirt entering. Undo the banjo screw of the leak-off pipe and move it to one side, taking care to retain the sealing washers. Undo the nuts or clamps that secure the atomiser and it should then be possible to prise it carefully from its seating, either using the manufacturer's special tool or a thick screwdriver. Remove and retain the copper joint ring (washer) on which the injector seats. Some engines do not have a copper washer, and in some it can be replaced the wrong way round, so check its position on removal. Block off the hole in the cylinder head with a clean piece of rag. If the injector sticks in place, a little penetrating oil around the sides may help. If it still defies withdrawal the compression of the engine can be used. Replace the securing nuts so that they are only slightly loose, pull the engine stop control to prevent it starting, and crank the engine over on the starter, when the compression in the cylinder should do the trick. If this fails, but only in a real emergency situation, the engine can be allowed to start, but stand well clear and stop it immediately.

If no replacement injector is available it is possible to carry out a rudimentary check with the injector on the engine. Reconnect the high-pressure fuel pipe and make some arrangement to collect the spray, making sure that this cannot be accidentally ignited. The importance of keeping your body well clear of the spray is emphasised again. Slack back the union nuts on the other injectors so that the engine cannot start, and crank it over on the starter. There should be a fine, equal spray from each hole of the nozzle without visible streaks of unatomised fuel, and there should be a distinct start and end to each delivery, with no sign of dribble from the nozzle which indicates leakage of the needle valve on its seat. Check also that there is no leakage at the nozzle nut joint.

It may sometimes be sufficient to clean off any carbon deposit from the outside of the nozzle and to clear the holes with a strand of copper wire (not steel wire, which will damage the holes). If that fails the injector must be returned for servicing. If no spare is held, replace the defective one on the engine and connect it up in all respects as before. A

four-cylinder engine will run satisfactorily at low powers with one cylinder out of action, sufficient to get you home. Attempting to dismantle an atomiser without the necessary tools, equipment and technical data is not recommended.

When fitting a spare atomiser the hole in the cylinder head must be clean, and a new sealing washer should be used if available since the copper hardens in use. If this is a problem, the old washer can be annealed over a flame to a dull red heat and then quenched in cold water. The atomiser must be squarely seated and tightened down evenly, with a final check when the engine is running.

High-pressure fuel pipes need careful handling. Their unions are fitted with brass olives or nipples which deform under pressure to make the joint, and which should not be overtightened. In the event of leakage examine the olive to see that there is a good contact line around it, and that it is tight on the pipe. Good alignment of the pipe is essential, and whatever clamps that are fitted to reduce vibration must be tightened and inspected periodically. If it is necessary to fit a spare pipe, use the right one for that cylinder, since they are made not just to fit but also to be the correct length for individual cylinders which affects the injection timing.

Finally connect up the banjo bolt of the leak-off pipe, using new washers if available. When the engine is running check round all the connections and tighten or refit as required.

VENTING THE FUEL SYSTEM

Mention was made earlier of the need to vent (or bleed) the fuel system if air gets in – due to maintenance, leakage on the suction side, or running out of fuel. Even a small amount of air can cause problems with many types of injection pumps, but some modern ones are to a degree self-venting. Systems vary, but every owner of a diesel-engined boat should know the procedure for venting his own fuel system, and exactly where the different vent screws are. The procedure is quite simple if one remembers to work from low pressure to high pressure – that is in the direction of the fuel flow.

First make sure that there is sufficient fuel in the tank. The fuel is drawn from here through the primary filter by the lift pump, so see that there are no obvious leaks on this part of the system, where air might be sucked in. On most engines there is a handle immediately below the lift pump which can be pumped up and down for manual operation. Should there be no stroke on this handle the engine has stopped so that the diaphragm in the pump is fully depressed, and the engine will have to be turned about half a revolution to make manual operation possible. Many other engines have a plunger-type pump, whose plunger must be unscrewed before it can be operated manually, while a few engines have no external lift pump, but one which is incorporated with the injection pump or one of the filters, or somewhere else in the system.

Clean off the area round each vent screw or union involved, to make certain that no dirt can get into the system. Slacken the vent screw (or, if not fitted, the fuel outlet pipe connection) on the secondary filter – as at A in Fig 3. Operate the pump until fuel flows out steadily, with no air bubbles, and then close the vent screw or connection. A bowl or a plastic bag can be used to catch the emerging fuel and prevent it falling in the bilge. If there is another filter before the injection pump, then this must be vented in similar fashion. Most injection pumps have two vent screws (in which case the lower one is vented first), but some have only one. Details should be given in the engine handbook. In each case operate the lift pump until all traces of air have disappeared.

Finally it is necessary to clear any air from the fuel pipes to the atomisers. Loosen the pipe union at each atomiser, make sure that the engine stop control is set to the running position, apply full throttle, and crank the engine over on the starter until air-free fuel emerges at each union – when the union is retightened. This should not take more than half a minute, which is about the maximum time that a starter motor should be operated continuously. Smaller engines fitted with decompressors can be turned over by hand for this operation, which will save not only the starter but also the battery, which may already be low if previous attempts have been made to start the engine. Once air-free fuel reaches the atomisers the engine should start as normal, whereupon all vent screws and unions on the system must be checked for leakage.

Although not so important as clean fuel, the air which is ingested in considerable quantities by a diesel needs to be as free as possible of solid particles, so filters are as necessary for diesels as they are for petrol engines.

TURBOCHARGERS

In a naturally aspirated engine the amount of fuel that can be burned efficiently in the cylinder depends on the weight of air that can be drawn into it. This can be increased by fitting a turbocharger – a small turbine driven by the exhaust gases and connected on the same shaft to a centrifugal blower which pumps air into the inlet manifold.

To match the extra air supplied, the fuel injection equipment will need to deliver more fuel, and there are other factors to consider such as improved cooling arrangements and stronger working parts for the additional power developed. If these matters are taken care of, the power can be increased by upwards of 50 per cent, although there are penalties in terms of general cost and complexity.

There is a limit to the degree of turbocharging because at a certain point the increased back pressure of the exhaust gases becomes counter-productive. Another problem is that as the turbocharger increases the air pressure so it raises its temperature, thus reducing its density and the weight of air supplied. So it is common to fit a charge cooler (often called an intercooler or aftercooler) which reduces the air's temperature and increases its density before it enters the manifold.

Turbochargers run at high speed (100,000rpm or more) and at high temperatures so they are usually fitted with a heat shield. Good lubrication is needed, and a turbocharged engine should not be highly revved immediately after starting before the oil pressure has built up in the turbocharger bearings. For the same reason, the engine should not be shut down suddenly from high revolutions because the turbocharger will go on spinning after the lubricating oil pressure has dropped to zero.

At low engine speeds the turbocharger speed drops and the volume of air (or boost) provided is reduced. Under these conditions the supply of fuel to the engine must be restricted to prevent emission of black smoke. This is the function of the boost control unit, or 'smoke-limiter', fitted to the governor of the injection pump. When the manifold pressure drops to a certain figure it restricts the amount of fuel delivered to the engine.

5. LUBRICATION AND CORROSION

Oils and additives – Four-stroke engines – Changing oil – Two-stroke engines – Grease – Corrosion

Lubrication separates moving surfaces by a film of material which shears easily and offers minimal frictional resistance. Lubricants may also take heat away from moving parts and inhibit corrosion. In an internal combustion engine they help to maintain a gas-tight seal between the piston and the cylinder wall, and remove combustion products from the internal surfaces.

Under ideal running conditions a fluid film of oil separates the bearing surfaces, and is sufficiently thick to prevent physical contact between them. When a journal (shaft) starts to rotate in a bearing, oil spirals up the shaft until it builds up sufficient pressure to hold the two surfaces apart. This 'fluid film' or 'wedge' lubrication depends on sufficient speed of rotation, the maintenance of correct clearances, and oil of the right type and cleanliness. It cannot be sustained during starting or stopping, or if the speed is too low, or if the loading is too heavy. Then it is necessary to resort to what is called 'boundary lubrication' – for example where gear teeth mesh, special extreme pressure (EP) oils are required to maintain lubrication.

OILS AND ADDITIVES

Modern engines make big demands on the lubricants they use, to maximise their power from a given size and weight. So oil, for diesel engines in particular, contains important additives to improve certain characteristics.

Viscosity (the thickness of an oil) is an important factor – determining how the oil flows through the engine, the thickness of the oil film in bearings and the load they can carry. The choice of viscosity is a compromise to give easy starting from cold, rapid film formation, good running performance, and low consumption.

As an oil is heated its viscosity drops – it gets thinner – and additives are used to reduce this tendency (or to improve the viscosity index). Viscosity is measured on a numerical scale originated by the Society of Automotive Engineers in America. SAE 20, SAE 30 and SAE 40, in ascending 'thickness', are grades of viscosity specified at 210°F (99°C) – a typical running temperature. The suffix W denotes an oil recommended for winter use, and SAE 5W, SAE 10W and SAE 20W are oils which stay 'thin' at low temperatures, with their viscosities specified at 0°F (18°C). A multigrade oil has a viscosity which changes less with alterations of temperature. Thus a 20W-50 oil has a viscosity within the SAE 20W grade at 0°F, but a viscosity of SAE 50 at 210°F – combining the properties required for low temperature starting and high temperature running.

Other additives are used to improve detergency and dispersancy (to keep the engine clean inside), to reduce oxidation and the formation of deposits on pistons and rings, to prevent acidic compounds causing corrosion, to reduce foaming, and to reduce wear due to scuffing on cams and tappets. All these additives are gradually used up, so it is important to change the oil at specified intervals – typically after about 200 hours running.

Only an oil as specified in the maker's handbook should be used for engine lubrication. A different viscosity may be needed for special conditions – for example, in the tropics. It is vital that the oil is clean, so store it only in sealed containers and check filling funnels before use.

If you are unsure what oil to use, and in the absence of reliable information, be guided by the specification marked on the can. There are two main international classifications for engine oil, using letters to indicate an ascending order of quality. One is the US military specification (MIL-L-2104C and MIL-L-46152 for example, either being suitable for four-stroke petrol engines and normally aspirated diesels, but the former being preferred for turbocharged diesels). The other is a system devised by the American Petroleum Institute (API) in which the quality is designated as CC or CD for diesel engines (CD being the better), and SE or SF for petrol engines (SF being better).

Two-stroke petrol engines have different requirements which are discussed below and in chapter 9.

Gearboxes too have their own particular needs, and the correct lubricant should be found from the engine handbook.

FOUR-STROKE ENGINES

A diagram of the lubricating system of a typical four-stroke engine, whether petrol or diesel, is shown in Fig 1. The oil pump draws from near the bottom of the sump (possibly through a strainer) and close to it is a relief valve which returns surplus oil to the sump once the required pressure is reached. This varies with individual engines and operating conditions, but should be about 30-60lb/in^2 (2.1–4.2kg/cm^2).

Most marine engines have an oil cooler through which raw (sea or river) water passes from the cooling system. From the cooler the oil is piped to the oil filter which has a renewable element. Modern practice is for the full flow of oil to pass through the filter, but in some older engines only a proportion of the oil is filtered each time it circulates. The filter may have a by-pass which opens when the element cannot accept the full flow – when the oil is cold and thick, or if the filter is blocked.

From the filter the oil is led back inside the crankcase to the main oil gallery or pressure rail which runs the length of the crankshaft and feeds the main bearings. Oilways drilled through the crankshaft webs supply oil to the big end bearings, and surplus oil drains into the sump. An oil seal prevents leakage at the rear end, while at the front there is a connection to lubricate the timing gears. A separate supply goes to the rocker shaft for the valve gear on top of the head.

Lubrication of the cylinders, pistons and rings is vital. In smaller engines this is usually by splash from the big end bearings as they rotate. In larger engines each connecting rod is drilled to convey oil to the small end bush, and this supply may also cool the underside of the piston crown. A separate line feeds the turbocharger (where fitted) and this may have an additional filter.

Two important items deserving special attention are the dipstick to check the oil level in the sump, and the oil pressure gauge. Always check the oil level before starting, however inconvenient this may be. On a long passage it may be necessary to stop at some stage for this purpose. If the oil is always replenished midway between the full and empty marks on the dipstick it is easier to check consumption against running hours, which may give early indication of impending trouble. It is also easier to detect any rise of level. If a rise in oil level is accompanied by a loss of coolant in a fresh-water (indirect) cooling system, the two are probably related and may be due to a leaking cylinder head gasket, a leaking seal on a wet liner, or perhaps a crack in a cylinder head or wet liner. Such leaks are hard to trace, and require removal of the head.

Some diesels have high-pressure fuel pipes running to injectors under the valve cover on top of the head. A leak here will allow fuel to drain into the sump, but this should be easy to spot and rectify.

Other factors can influence the level in the sump. At low speeds some unburnt fuel may pass the pistons and get down into the sump, causing an apparent increase in oil level, but after a decent run on load this fuel will vaporise and the level return to normal. Also in the combustion process water is created, and although most of it leaves with the exhaust gases some may pass into the sump. Here it can mix with the products of combustion and turn acidic, although an additive is included in the lubricating oil to counter this.

An accurate oil pressure gauge is a prime requirement. Lights which indicate somewhat vaguely

Fig 1. Lubrication system of four-stroke engines: (1) oil strainer near bottom of sump; (2) oil pump; (3) pressure release valve; (4) oil cooler; (5) oil filter; (6) oil gallery; (7) oil feed to main bearing; (8) oil feed through crankshaft to big end bearing; (9) oil feed through connecting rod to small end bush and gudgeon pin; (10) oil feed to valve gear; (11) dipstick; (12) sump pump; (13) sump drain plug.

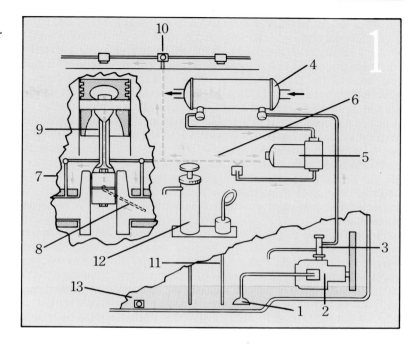

whether the pressure is (or is not) satisfactory are no substitute for a proper gauge from which it is possible to discern variations in pressure. The addition of an oil temperature gauge is a bonus.

In the event of a drop in oil pressure the most likely cause is lack of oil in the sump. Otherwise, the filter element may be dirty and overdue for renewal; the engine may be overheating, causing a decrease in viscosity which can be checked against the temperature gauges; oil of the wrong viscosity may have been used; the oil may be contaminated with water or fuel; the gauge may be defective (although the mechanical type is normally very reliable); the pressure relief valve may not be seated properly, perhaps due to dirt; the oil pump may be defective, although this is more likely to manifest itself by a gradual deterioration in performance; or if the engine has not been serviced at the specified intervals there may be a build-up of sludge restricting the flow in some parts of the system, such as the oil cooler. A gradual decline in oil pressure over a long time is normal, associated with general wear of bearings, but a rapid drop, especially accompanied by new and unusual engine sounds, points to a bearing failure.

CHANGING OIL

Luckily most of these problems can be prevented by proper maintenance. Nearly half of all bearing failures are due to dirty lubricating oil, so changing the oil and renewing the filter element are second in importance only to maintaining the oil level. Both these items will be included in the engine manufacturer's service recommendations, usually at about 200 hours running or once a season. As a basic rule, always remove oil when laying up for the winter.

First run the engine for several minutes until it is at operating temperature and the oil is warm. This makes it much easier to pump out, either using a pump attached to the engine, or a portable pump with a small diameter suction pipe through the dipstick hole. Suitable cans are needed so that the dirty oil can be taken ashore and disposed of at a garage, boatyard, or a council rubbish tip.

The quantity of oil required to refill will be given in the engine handbook – typically about a gallon (5l) for a 30hp (22kW) engine up to about 15 gallons (68l) for a 500hp (373kW). A similar amount should be carried on board as spare. Try to get as much of the dirty oil out as possible. It may help to turn the engine over a few revolutions on the starter, but take care that it cannot start.

Take a look at the used oil as it is removed. It should be quite black in colour, showing that the additives have been doing their work. A grey colour indicates the presence of water, which must be investigated.

Modern oil filters are screwed in place. Before removing them, clean off the housing and the surrounding area, and make sure that you have a replacement element. Use a chain or strap wrench to unscrew the filter, or pierce the side of the canister with a screwdriver to use as a lever. A large plastic bag around the filter will catch most of the oil that leaks from it as it is removed. Put the old element aside in order to discard it ashore, and clean the filter head with a lint-free cloth. Fit a new rubber joint ring to the housing, having removed the old one. Lubricate the ring with clean oil, and screw the new element into place. Don't overtighten; but screw up another half turn after resistance is felt.

Fill the engine with the new lubricating oil, making sure that any funnel used is scrupulously clean. Note that some engines which operate on what is called the 'dry sump' principle may require a special technique for filling, whereby the engine is first filled to the mark on the dipstick, run for a short period, and then topped up to the mark. On completion run the engine in order to check that there is no leak at the filter.

Record the date and engine hours at which the oil and filter were changed in the maintenance log, and replenish the stock of lubricating oil.

TWO-STROKE ENGINES

Two-stroke outboard engines rely on a very different principle for lubrication – the oil is mixed with the petrol and passes into the engine with it. This 'once-through, total loss' method of lubrication requires quite a different oil from that used in four-stroke engines. It must mix well with the fuel, and not separate out, which would cause a mixture either too rich in oil (resulting in exhaust smoke and plugs oiling up) or too weak (causing possible mechanical damage). Lighter oils mix better, but heavier ones are better lubricants and drain less readily from bearing surfaces when the engine is standing.

Once the fuel/oil mixture enters the crankcase, the fuel vaporises in the higher temperature. Some of the oil is deposited on the moving parts, while the rest is carried through into the combustion chamber to lubricate the cylinder bores and piston rings. Some gets burnt with the fuel, so detergent additives are needed to reduce deposits in combustion chambers and around exhaust ports, and to encourage combustion products to be swept out with the exhaust gases. Other additives reduce the oxidation of the oil, which otherwise forms a varnish-like layer on pistons and rings; neutralise acids formed by exhaust gas condensation; and prevent internal corrosion.

The correct fuel/oil mixture for an engine is determined by the manufacturer, and may be anything from 10:1 to 100:1. It used to be the practice with all two-stroke outboards to mix the correct amount of oil in the fuel tank – a process always subject to error. Now all the more powerful engines have separate tanks for petrol and oil, and the correct proportion of oil is automatically injected into the fuel before it enters the carburettor. This system is steadily being extended into lower-powered outboards as well. The details and the degree of sophistication vary with different makes but, in a typical engine, the fuel/oil mixture varies automatically from about 100:1 when idling to 50:1 when running at full power. An alarm may be fitted to sound when the oil reservoir needs refilling.

Whatever type of outboard you have, you should try to use the oil specified in the engine handbook. If for some reason that actual brand is not available, go for an outboard engine oil which is certified as TC-W by the (American) Boating Industry Association (BIA). TC-W stands for two-cycle (i.e. two-stroke) water-cooled. Secondly, if you have to mix the oil into the petrol for your engine, take great care to achieve the right proportions. Most manufacturers specify double the quantity of oil for a new engine, during the first few hours of running.

When mixing the fuel and oil, determine how much oil has to be added for a full tank. Start with a small quantity of petrol, add the oil and shake the tank thoroughly to get a good mix, and only then add the rest of the fuel. If a tank of mixture has been left standing for any time, it should be given a very good shake before it is put into use.

GREASE

Some parts of the boat's machinery may be lubricated by grease, which has several advantages as a lubricant. It is more likely to stay put than oil, being less affected by gravity and centrifugal force, and it does not drip or splash. Apart from lubricating it acts as a seal, protecting bearings from water or dirt. Because it tends to stay on bearing surfaces it reduces starting friction, and provides better protection to bearings subject to shock loads or to changes in direction. For the same reason it helps to prevent corrosion. Grease can operate over a wider range of temperature than any specific oil, but it does not disperse heat from a bearing as oil does.

Grease is used more for ball and roller bearings than for plain bearings. Only a relatively small quantity is needed to give adequate lubrication for ball and roller races, and too much will result in churning of the grease and a rise in temperature. As a general rule the bearing itself should be packed with grease, but the housing not more than half full.

Greases are grouped according to the thickening agent used. Those with a calcium or lime base are of a smooth texture and are resistant to water, but they are not suitable for temperatures above 120°F (50°C). Sodium-based greases can be used for higher temperatures but are not water-resistant and should not be used in a marine environment. Lithium-based greases are the most versatile – smooth, water-resistant, and effective at temperatures up to 250°F (120°C). They are used in many situations, from sterntube bearings to engine controls.

CORROSION

Boat engines (and other mechnical items on board) operate in a hostile environment – in a damp atmosphere and exposed to salt water – and are often left idle and neglected for weeks on end. Corrosion is more likely to destroy the average boat engine than any number of running hours under normal conditions, so it is important to understand what causes it, and how it can be prevented or minimised.

Substantial parts of most engines are made from cast iron or steel, both of which rust (oxidise) in a damp atmosphere unless protected. So other materials, mostly alloys (mixtures of metals) are used for working parts and where special mechanical properties are needed. Other ferrous metals (derived from iron) mostly corrode rapidly in a damp or salty atmosphere, but they have comparatively high

	NOBLE (PROTECTED) END VOLTAGE
Stainless steel (Type 316) passive	− 0.05
Monel	− 0.08
Stainless steel (Type 304) passive	− 0.08
Titanium	− 0.15
Stainless steel (Type 316) active	− 0.18
Silicon Bronze	− 0.18
Copper	− 0.24
Manganese Bronze	− 0.27
Admiralty Brass	− 0.29
Stainless steel (Type 304) active	− 0.53
Lead	− 0.55
Grey cast iron	− 0.61
Mild steel	− 0.61
Aluminium	− 0.75
Aluminium alloy 3003	− 0.94
Zinc	− 1.03
Galvanised steel	− 1.05
Magnesium alloys	− 1.6

Fig 2. The galvanic series in sea water. Those metals close together on the table have little effect on each other when in contact. Stainless steel appears in two places – passive where its oxide film is formed, and active where the film is not intact.

Fig 3. Corrosion cell with two dissimilar metals in an electrolyte, showing current flow. The same principle is used with sacrificial anodes (zinc in sea water) to protect underwater fittings. The zinc anode is continually eroded and has to be renewed periodically.

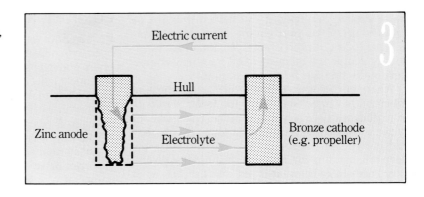

strengths and high melting points. Some non-ferrous metals corrode less but are relatively weak, and most have such low melting points that they are unsuitable for high temperatures.

Corrosion is an electrochemical process which requires a source of current, an electrolyte (such as sea water) and oxygen. The source of current may be 'external', caused by leakage currents from poorly-installed electrical systems (in which case the corrosion is called 'electrolytic'), or it may be generated by a difference in electrical potential between one metal and another ('galvanic'). Few metals are perfectly homogeneous, so minute currents can be created even within a single piece of metal by differences between one part of its surface and another.

Galvanic corrosion is very much worse, however, if two dissimilar metals are involved. Current will flow from one to the other through the electrolyte – as shown in Fig 3 – driven by a voltage corresponding to the difference between the potentials of the two metals given in the galvanic table (Fig 2).

Obviously metals close together in the table will have less effect on each other than metals further apart, but another important factor is the relative area of the two metals. If the area of the anode exposed to the electrolyte is small compared to the area of cathode, then corrosion will be worse.

In the case of some of the more corrosion-resistant metals and alloys, some protection is given by a thin oxide film on the surface, which excludes the necessary oxygen and electrolyte.

Corrosion is reduced by insulating dissimilar metals from each other and by keeping the electrolyte away with a sound coating of paint.

Sacrificial anodes, usually a special alloy of zinc or magnesium, may be fitted to protect underwater fittings such as seacocks and propellers. Zinc (or magnesium) is chosen because it is at the anodic end of the table and is attacked before other normal metals. They must always be left unpainted.

Even where cathodic protection is fitted, corrosion can occur if there are leakage currents from the boat's electrical system. The electrics must have a properly insulated return (not to earth as in a car), with a main isolating switch for the battery.

Corrosion is taking place unseen inside the engine for a number of reasons. When fuel is burnt water vapour is formed: much of this leaves with the exhaust gases, some finds its way into the crankcase, and condenses there when the engine is cold. So rusting can occur on metal surfaces even though it is discouraged by additives in the lubricating oil. Water can also react with air and sulphur from diesel fuel to form sulphurous acid which will attack metal surfaces. Both these situations can occur when an engine is started and run on light load for only a few minutes, so avoid doing this.

Another source of engine damage is condensation in the fuel tank, especially with diesel engines and their sensitive fuel injection equipment. Condensation can be reduced by keeping the tanks as full as possible. Water can get into the engine in other ways – through the exhaust pipe, a leaking cylinder head gasket or a leaking water pump seal for example.

6. COOLING AND INSTALLATION

Indirect cooling – Overheating – Installation – Ventilation – Noise reduction – Exhaust systems – Controls – Instruments

Most marine engines are water-cooled but there are a few low powered units which rely on air cooling by means of suitable ducting and a fan. Air-cooled engines are more noisy because they lack the surrounding water jacket, but they have the merit of simplicity and little can go wrong unless somebody blocks the air duct. In addition, there is no water to drain off for winter lay-ups.

About a third of the heat generated from the fuel has to be removed by the cooling system, so correct functioning is important or overheating may result in expensive damage. The simplest, lightest, and cheapest method is to use the water in which the boat is floating, in a direct (or raw-water) cooling system like that in Fig 1. The circulating pump draws water through a strainer and delivers it to the oil cooler, through the cooling passages in the cylinder block and head, round the exhaust manifold, and then overboard (usually through the exhaust pipe).

This, however, is not very satisfactory on several counts. Firstly, even though it passes through a strainer, the water carries impurities such as weed or silt which accumulate in water passages. Secondly, it is difficult to regulate the temperature satisfactorily. In order to prevent the deposition of salt on internal surfaces it is necessary to keep the water temperature below about 140°F (60°C). This is too cold for efficient operation of the engine and can also cause contamination of the lubricating oil

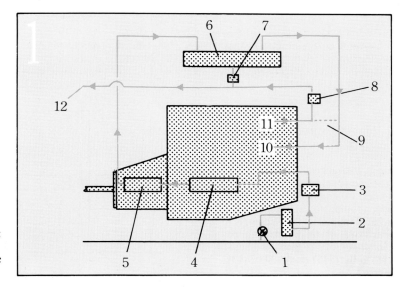

Fig 1. Direct cooling system: (1) seacock; (2) strainer; (3) raw-water pump; (4) engine oil cooler; (5) gearbox oil cooler; (6) exhaust manifold; (7) relief valve, to provide circulation through manifold when thermostat is closed; (8) thermostat; (9) by-pass; (10) water inlet to block and head; (11) outlet; (12) discharge overboard.

by water condensing in the cylinder. Finally, the flow of corrosive hot sea water through the engine restricts the use of materials that can be employed.

INDIRECT COOLING

So the great majority of engines are fitted with indirect (heat-exchanger) cooling. A separate pump circulates clean, fresh water to cool the engine, and this water is cooled in turn by raw water in a heat exchanger. A diagrammatic layout is shown in Fig 2.

The fresh-water temperature is controlled by a thermostat, which allows it to reach a higher temperature for more efficient engine operation. A pressure cap (similar to that on a car radiator) on the heat exchanger prevents water losses due to evaporation, but serves as a safety valve if the temperature or pressure rise too far. As the fresh water is in a sealed circuit, it is possible to add corrosion inhibitors and anti-freeze to the coolant.

Routine maintenance is fairly simple. First and foremost: keep the inlet strainer clean. It should always be inspected before getting under way, having first made sure that its seacock is closed. On many modern installations it is quite possible to

remove the strainer with the seacock open, but it is best to make a practice of closing the seacock before working on the raw-water system and whenever the boat is unattended. Remember to open it before starting the engine, though! If possible, check the flow of cooling water overboard once the engine is running, and watch the cooling-water temperature.

The raw-water pump will probably be driven off the front of the engine, and is likely to be of the Jabsco type with a neoprene impeller (see Fig 3). This has several blades mounted slightly off centre in a circular housing. As the impeller rotates, the blades distort and provide a self-priming pumping action. The pump depends on liquid for lubrication and must not be run dry for more than a few seconds. It is wise to carry a spare impeller, which can be fitted quite easily by removing the front cover. Make sure that the replacement impeller is fitted with the blades deflected in the right direction – that is trailing from the direction of rotation. A touch of grease, glycerine, or washing-up liquid will assist insertion, and lubricate the pump until it fills with water on first starting.

Every flexible hose joint in the system should be secured by two stainless steel hose clips. These, and

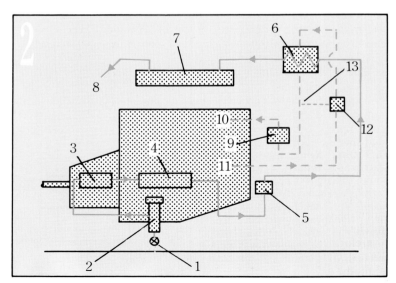

Fig 2. Indirect cooling system: (1) seacock; (2) strainer; (3) gearbox oil cooler; (4) engine oil cooler; (5) raw-water pump; (6) heat exchanger; (7) exhaust manifold; (8) discharge overboard; (9) fresh-water pump; (10) water inlet to block and head; (11) outlet; (12) thermostat; (13) by-pass.

Fig 3. Operation of Jabsco pump. The flexible neoprene impeller rotates anticlockwise. On leaving the offset plate at the top an impeller blade straightens, and creates a partial vacuum, so drawing in liquid through the inlet port top left. As the impeller rotates each blade in turn carries the liquid through the pump. When the blades again contact the offset plate they bend with a squeezing action to give a continuous discharge from the outlet port on the right.

the hoses themselves, need to be examined regularly, and replaced when they start to deteriorate.

The fresh-water pump will probably be belt driven, together with the alternator, and is not likely to give trouble so long as the belt tension is checked from time to time. Firm finger pressure in the middle of the longest run of the belt should cause between ¼in (6mm) and ½in (12mm) deflection. A spare belt should be carried.

The level of coolant in the header tank or heat exchanger needs more regular attention. It should be kept topped up with fresh water just like a car radiator. But beware: when the engine has been running the header tank will be under pressure – and the water is *very* hot! Any regular loss of coolant points to a leak somewhere in the system, which demands investigation.

Just occasionally the thermostat gives trouble. The old type, operated by a bellows, 'failed safe' by opening and overcooling the engine, but the more modern wax-capsule types close when they fail and therefore cause overheating. The thermostat can be tested by heating it slowly in a pan of water – it should start to open at about 175°F (80°C). If it does not function the engine can run without it until a spare can be fitted.

OVERHEATING

From all this, it should be evident what to do if the engine temperature starts to rise. First slow right down. Nine times out of ten the trouble will be in the sea inlet strainer. If the strainer is clear, check the raw-water pump.

Should no problem emerge with the raw-water circuit check the belt drive to the fresh-water pump. Stop the engine, let it cool, take the necessary precautions and check the level of coolant in the header tank. If this is satisfactory suspect the thermostat or the fresh-water pump itself.

If an engine has seriously overheated, some of the water in the header tank will have boiled off. This will have to be replaced, but allow the engine to cool before doing so, otherwise the cold water may crack the head or block. Frost too can damage water systems, which need particular attention when it comes to laying up for winter (see chapter 11).

In addition to a temperature gauge, some installations have an audible or visual alarm to indicate high water temperature, which is a useful feature. Automatic shut-down arrangements, however, are not appropriate for marine engines – the consequences of the engine stopping unexpectedly could be far more serious than the possibly minor overheating which triggered it.

Heat from the fresh-water circuit of an indirect-cooling system can be used in a calorifier to provide hot water, cabin heating, or to operate a desalinisation plant to produce fresh water.

INSTALLATION

Even the best and most expensive engine will not operate satisfactorily unless it is properly installed. Several requirements have to be met, some of which need checking and attention throughout the life of the boat. Some of the more important aspects of engine installation are shown in Fig 4.

The attitude of the engine is important, because

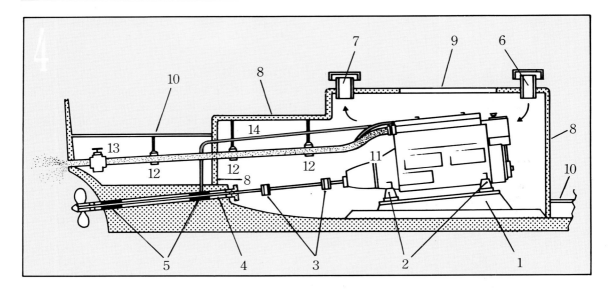

Fig 4. Engine installation: (1) engine bearers; (2) flexible mountings (four); (3) flexible shaft couplings; (4) sterngland; (5) sterntube bearings (water lubricated); (6) air inlet; (7) air outlet; (8) sound insulation incorporating resilient layer, heavy barrier material, absorbent foam and protective skin; (9) close-fitting access hatch; (10) sound insulation; (11) water injection bend; (12) clips to support exhaust hose; (13) exhaust shut-off valve; (14) cooling-water supply for sterntube lubrication.

it will have been designed to operate within certain limits of fore-and-aft inclination, and certain angles of heel. In a motor boat the trim can change under way, as does the heel of a sailing boat.

Engine bearers need to be strong and rigid, and to extend well forward and aft to spread the load of the engine. Apart from the actual weight of the machinery and the thrust of the propeller, bearers and mountings must be able to withstand the acceleration forces that are experienced in a seaway.

Nowadays most engines, particularly in pleasure craft, are flexibly mounted to reduce the vibration and noise passed to the rest of the boat, and to absorb shocks and distortion of the hull, which would otherwise stress the engine. Flexible mounts normally include a height adjustment which is a

great help when finally aligning the engine and the propeller shaft in a conventional layout. If an engine is flexibly mounted, then flexibility must be arranged for everything connected to it – shafting, piping, exhaust and controls.

If the propeller shaft passes through a shaft log with rigid bearings and a fixed sterngland at the forward end, then there must be flexible couplings between it and gearbox output.

An alternative arrangement is to eliminate bearings in the shaft log, with only the outboard end of the propeller shaft being supported by the P-bracket immediately forward of the propeller. In this case the sterngland is supported by a length of reinforced hose to give it the necessary flexibility. The big drawback of this is that if the hose splits or comes loose the boat will be flooded.

Although a new form of sterngland depends upon maintaining a small axial clearance to keep out the water, most boats have a conventional stuffing box which contains turns (rings) of special packing round the shaft, compressed on to it by a nut or gland at the forward end. A slight drip of water must be expected, and indeed encouraged. It is a mistake to overtighten the gland, which is then liable to overheat and damage the shaft, making it increasingly difficult to achieve a reasonable seal.

Sterntube bearings may be plain white metal, grease lubricated and requiring periodic attention, but increasingly common are fluted rubber (cutless) bearings which are water lubricated – usually from the engine's raw-water cooling system. P-bracket bearings are almost always of the cutless type, lubricated by the water which surrounds them.

Flexible couplings are no substitute for accurate alignment between the propeller shaft and the gearbox output. This is measured with feeler gauges between the mating surfaces at the coupling, and should be done with the boat in the water and all normal fuel, water and stores on board. Since the hull can change shape slightly and flexible engine mountings can settle a bit with age, it is advisable to check this alignment annually.

VENTILATION

An engine needs a large amount of air, not only for combustion but to ventilate the surrounding space, to keep it cool and to disperse any fumes from the engine or from battery charging. But the air supply arrangements must keep out any water (even in a heavy sea when the spray is flying) and should not prejudice whatever attempts are made to reduce the level of noise emitted by the machinery into other parts of the boat.

For safety reasons petrol-engined boats demand special attention to ventilation by means of a sealed extraction fan that will draw from the bottom of the engine space. This should invariably be run for several minutes before starting the engine to make sure that any petrol fumes are extracted. It helps to have a reminder notice to this effect close by the ignition and starter switch.

Your engines may not seem quite as crisp and powerful as usual on a hot summer's day, and there is good reason for this. A rise of temperature from 68°F (20°C) to 104°F (40°C), for example, in the engine space will reduce the power output by 10 per cent simply due to the reduced density of the combustion air. This effect can be reduced by arranging trunking to feed relatively cool air from outside the boat to the engines' air intakes, rather than making the engines breathe the hot air which surrounds them.

NOISE REDUCTION

Engine noise reduction now receives more attention from boatbuilders, and can be tackled in various ways.

First, engine vibration can be isolated from the rest of the boat by using flexible mountings, flexible shaft couplings, and resilient pipes connected to the engine. Second, the engine space can be enclosed by sound insulating and absorbing material, with openings suitably baffled. There are proprietary materials available for this, but as they need to be fire resistant and impervious to oil and water, they are quite expensive. Other surfaces inside the boat such as the cabin floor and roof also benefit from sound absorbing materials. Third, some structural materials such as steel and aluminium can be damped by bonding on a layer of material to reduce their resonance.

EXHAUST SYSTEMS

Getting exhaust gases out of the engine and safely over the side presents other problems. Note the word 'safely' – exhaust gases contain lethal carbon monoxide, so that even the smallest leak within the boat can be very dangerous, and exhaust fumes should be discouraged from blowing back into the accommodation. For reasons of efficiency the exhaust back pressure needs to be kept to a minimum, so the pipe should be of good size and as short as possible with few bends.

There are two distinct systems – dry and wet. The former, very similar to a car exhaust, is not often found in pleasure craft but is the only feasible way for air-cooled engines. Since the exhaust pipe will get very hot it must be well lagged or jacketed, some allowance must be made for expansion, and there must be some form of trap to stop condensation running back along the exhaust pipe and into the engine.

Wet exhausts are almost universal in pleasure

craft, with raw water from the engine cooling system being discharged into the exhaust pipe close to the exhaust manifold, thus cooling the pipe and also helping to silence the noise from the exhaust. In order to avoid excessive back pressure, a proportion of the raw water may be discharged directly overboard in some installations, while some may be led to cool the sterntube bearings as previously described.

Often in motor boats the water injection bend (where the exhaust leaves the manifold or the turbocharger) joins an exhaust hose which leads with a steady fall in gradient and with or without a silencer to the transom, where it discharges roughly level with the waterline. It is seamanlike for some form of shut-off valve to be fitted at this point. This simple form of wet exhaust, as illustrated in Fig 4, is fitted in countless boats.

When the engine is installed with the exhaust manifold near to or below the waterline, as is often the case in auxiliary sailing craft for example, a special arrangement is needed to prevent any risk of water getting back into the engine. This may take the form of an elevated mixing chamber, above both the engine and waterline, where the cooling water and exhaust gases are mixed.

Alternatively a water-lock system may be fitted, as shown diagramatically in Fig 5. Here the cooling-water injection pipe is led in a loop well above the waterline, and at its highest point is either a vacuum relief valve or a bleed overboard through a small-bore pipe. (If this discharges through the topsides somewhere amidships it provides a good visual indication of the flow of cooling water). The function of the vacuum relief valve or bleed pipe is to eliminate any possibility of water being syphoned back into the engine. The exhaust gases and cooling water then pass down into the water-lock silencer chamber, which must have sufficient capacity to contain any water draining down into it from the two pipes connected to it when the engine is stopped. When the engine is running the water level in the chamber is as shown in the diagram – surplus water being forced overboard by the exhaust gases. Again it is advisable to have a shut-off valve at the skin fitting.

Due to the twin dangers of leaking exhaust fumes and of flooding by sea water, exhaust systems need regular inspection (which they seldom get because they are often inaccessible). Water injection bends are most liable to corrosion. Hose clips should be doubled up, and examined fre-

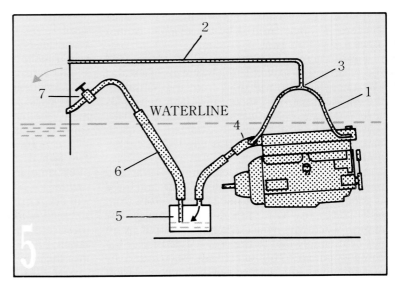

Fig 5. Water-lock exhaust system: (1) cooling-water pipe looped above waterline; (2) small-bore pipe for bleed overboard – as an alternative a vacuum relief valve may be fitted at (3); (4) water injection bend; (5) water-lock silencer chamber; (6) outlet pipe; (7) exhaust shut-off valve.

quently, while exhaust hoses can chafe on parts of the hull if they are not properly supported – there should be no sags where water can collect when the engine is shut down. Assuming a shut-off valve is fitted at the skin fitting, always close it while the boat is left unattended for any length of time – and remember to open it up when preparing for sea.

CONTROLS

Most boat engines have the following controls: (1) a starter/ignition switch, which for a diesel engine may be combined with some form of starting aid; (2) a throttle lever, controlling the output of the fuel pump of a diesel engine and the carburettor throttle of a petrol engine; (3) a lever controlling the ahead/neutral/astern operation of the gearbox; and (4) for diesel engines only, a 'stop' control. For petrol engines this function is performed by the ignition switch.

Modern practice is for (2), (3) and (4) to be performed by cable controls, which are efficient, easy to install and require little maintenance. For hydraulically operated gearboxes and smaller mechanical ones, (2) and (3) are often combined into a 'single-lever' control, which operates both the engine throttle and the gear change from one lever. This is seldom as smooth or precise as the twin-lever systems usually fitted to larger craft, in which separate levers are used for throttle and gear selection, but has the advantages of being easier to use and of automatically reducing the engine speed to idling before a change of gear is made – prolonging the life of the gearbox. When a button on the side of the pedestal is pushed in the lever can be moved forward to increase engine fuelling (e.g. for starting) without engaging ahead gear. In some controls the same effect is obtained using a separate 'run-up' lever which allows you to select a required idling speed before shifting out of neutral in order to prevent the engine stalling when cold.

Gearbox controls should be fitted with the correct 'handle sense': that is, the handle is pushed forward for ahead operation and pulled back to go astern. It is also important when manoeuvring that there are positive detents (notches) in the ahead/neutral/astern operation so that the operator can feel when the required position has been selected.

Push-pull control cables do not lend themselves to repair, and if problems develop it is simplest to fit a new cable. However, much can be done to extend their working life by making regular checks on connections and anchor points for security, by cleaning off salt deposits and dirt, and by lubricating the exposed moving parts regularly in order to minimise friction and prevent corrosion.

Visual inspection should cover all terminals and end fittings, seals, split pins and the like. Check rod ends for straightness and examine the jacket throughout its length for any sign of damage.

If the operation is not smooth throughout the whole range of movement, disconnect the cable at the 'receiving' end (the engine or gearbox) and check the movement. If it then functions satisfactorily, the trouble must lie at the receiving end rather than in the cable itself. If the control is still sticking, disconnect the 'transmitting' end as well to find out whether the trouble lies there or in the cable. On reassembly or replacement of a cable make certain that all fittings are correctly installed and tightened.

INSTRUMENTS

Engines are expensive items so they deserve good instruments to monitor their performance and safeguard them: tachometer (rev counter), oil pressure gauge, oil temperature gauge, coolant temperature gauge, voltmeter and fuel gauge are all desirable. Visual and audible alarms to signal low oil pressure and high coolant temperatures are useful additions. Depending on the installation a gearbox oil pressure gauge may be added, while a turbocharged engine needs a boost pressure gauge. A labour saving device, which avoids the need to keep records of engine operating times, is an engine hour meter.

Although there is something reassuring about 'mechanical' instruments (in which the tachometer, for example, is driven by a cable off the engine), modern instruments are electrical. They have the advantage that there is no limit to the

distance between the 'sender' on the engine and the instrument, and that one sender can feed two (or more) instruments at different locations. Installation is simplified with pre-wired looms from the engine senders and instrument panel terminating in multi-pin connections.

Attention needs to be given to the precise siting of instruments, so that they are easily visible from the helmsman's position. Panel lighting needs to be at a proper level for night operation. Modern thinking is that dim white lighting is more effective than red at preserving night vision, but in most boats (as with other installation matters) you may have to put up with whatever you have got.

7. TRANSMITTING THE POWER

Two-shaft gearboxes – Epicyclic gearboxes – Lubrication and
maintenance – Shafting – Propellers – Outdrives – Saildrives

The power of an engine has to be transformed into thrust in order to drive a boat through the water. There are several ways of doing this, the most common method being to connect the engine to a gearbox, which drives a propeller shaft extending aft and out of the hull to a propeller.

It is possible to have such an installation without a gearbox, but this incurs three penalties: the engine and propeller are directly connected so you have to stop the engines in order to stop the boat; very few engines will run backwards so there is no facility for astern power; and unless the engine is exceptionally slow-revving, it is unlikely that the propeller will be operating at its most efficient speed.

So the vast majority of craft with a conventional inboard engine installation have what is termed a reverse/reduction gearbox. This takes the revs produced by the engine, and reduces them – typically, by about a half – to a speed at which the propeller can operate efficiently. The gearbox also provides a means of making the propeller revolve in the opposite direction to the engine when required, or to remain still while the engine carries on turning, and transfers the thrust of the propeller to the boat.

Different configurations of gearbox, including some whose output shafts are lower than the input shaft (drop-centre), down-angled, or even point back under the engine (V-drives), give designers considerable flexibility in deciding on engine location.

Luckily the characteristics of a marine propeller only require a single gear ratio in order to get a boat moving from rest and take her up to maximum speed. This ratio needs to be carefully calculated depending on the designed speed of the boat, the maximum engine rpm and the diameter of propeller that can be fitted. To satisfy the theoretical requirements for propeller efficiency, the diameter should be as large as possible but this presents practical difficulties in any installation so that propeller design is something of a compromise – and often trial and error.

Generally, light high-speed planing craft will have direct-drive gearboxes (i.e. with no reduction ratio) swinging small propellers. Heavier planing hulls, semi-displacement and displacement boats require reduction ratios to an increasing degree; a reduction of 2:1, for example, doubles the torque in the propeller shaft and allows a bigger propeller to be swung, in order to give the necessary thrust to get a heavier planing boat on to the plane.

Having a gearbox naturally involves some loss in efficiency, depending on such factors as the type of gearbox, the amount of oil entrained and its viscosity and temperature, the torque transmitted, and the engine speed. At best a reverse/reduction gearbox is about 95 per cent efficient (at low engine speed) but this figure can drop to 90 per cent or less at higher rpm.

The several different makes of gearbox mostly fall into two categories. One includes layshaft and two-shaft boxes which operate on very similar principles, and the other is the epicyclic or planetary type.

TWO-SHAFT GEARBOXES

The principle of a two-shaft gearbox is explained in Fig 1. The input drive from the engine is shown at (1) and rotates constantly in one direction, as indicated by the arrow, while the engine is running. The input shaft has two gears mounted upon it, (2) and (5), which are spaced apart. Gear (2) engages directly with (3) to provide ahead transmission.

Astern rotation of the output shaft is provided by the gears (5), (6), and (7). Gear (5) engages with the intermediate gear (6), which in turn meshes with (7).

The manufacturer achieves the required reduction ratio by adjusting the sizes of (2), (3), (5) and (7).

Either (3) or (7) can be connected to the propeller shaft coupling (9) by means of a clutch situated between them. When the clutch is in its mid-position, neither (3) nor (7) are engaged so the gearbox is in neutral.

This type of gearbox lends itself to the employment of cone clutches where the final engagement is achieved by the thrust of the propeller shaft – either forward or aft as the case may be. These clutches are simple and effective, but there is no way of adjusting them and once they slip they need to be renewed.

Apart from wear over a very long period, the most common cause of damage is failure to throttle the engine back to idling speed before engaging or reversing the gearbox – and this in turn can be due to bad adjustment of a single lever control.

EPICYCLIC GEARBOXES

Despite appearances, the concept of an epicyclic gearbox (see Fig 2) is simple. The drive gear (1) (sometimes called the sun gear) engages with two or more pinion gears (2), which in turn drive spur gears (3). The pinion and spur (planetary gears) are carried in a cage which is free to revolve round the drive gear and is connected to the output shaft. The spur gears (3) engage with teeth around the inside of a ring gear or annulus (4). For ahead operation the drive gear, pinion and spur gears, and the annulus are all locked together and rotate as one unit in the same direction as the engine.

To go astern, the annulus is held stationary by a brake band (5), or by a clutch arrangement. The sun gear, driven by the engine, rotates in the same direction as before, hence driving the pinion gears in the opposite direction. These in turn drive the spur gears (the same way as the engine), which therefore run round the teeth on the inside of the stationary annulus. The pinion and spur gear

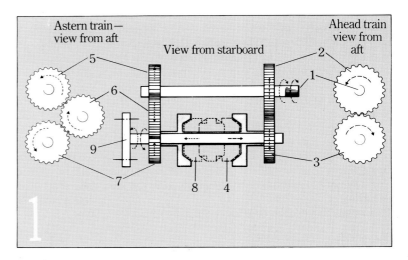

Fig 1. Diagrammatic arrangement of a two-shaft gearbox, with input top right and output bottom left: (1) input drive from engine; (2) and (3) ahead drive gears; (4) clutch in ahead position; (5), (6) and (7) astern drive train; (8) clutch in astern position; (9) shaft coupling.

Fig 2. Diagrammatic arrangement of
an epicyclic gearbox, with ahead
transmission on the right and astern
on the left: (1) drive or sun gear; (2)
pinion gears; (3) spur gears; (4)
annulus with internal gear teeth; (5)
brake band, shown in locked (astern)
position; (6) assembly which carries
pinion and spur gears, connected to
output shaft.

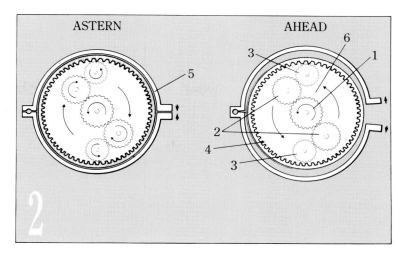

assembly are connected to the output shaft, driving
it in the reverse direction to that of the engine.

A bevel gearbox is a variant of the epicyclic type,
working on much the same principle.

As epicyclic gearboxes have more moving parts
than the two-shaft type, they cause greater power
losses, and need periodic adjustments to their
clutches and brake bands. Also, they sometimes
have a tendency to creep ahead in neutral due to oil
drag. This usually disappears once the oil warms
up, but it may demand care when first getting
under way. To counter these disadvantages, epicyclic gearboxes are much lighter and more compact than equivalent two-shaft units.

LUBRICATION AND MAINTENANCE

Although many small gearboxes are mechanically
operated, the clutches of larger and more sophisticated versions are usually operated hydraulically,
allowing the use of cable controls. Hydraulic gearboxes have their own oil pump, together with cooler
and filter. Gearbox lubrication systems are in any
case invariably separate from the engine lubrication
system and can therefore be kept clean and free
from combustion products. Often they require a
different lubricant. Details vary from make to make,
but there are some general rules:

(1) Use only the recommended lubricant. Depending on the make and type of gearbox this may
be engine oil, transmission fluid, or an extreme
pressure (EP) gear oil. Make sure it is perfectly
clean, and never mix different types or brands of
oil. Always clean round the dipstick area before
removing it, to avoid even the smallest particle of
dirt causing damage inside.

(2) Check the oil level regularly. In some cases
special instructions must be followed: it may, for
example, be important to check the level immediately after stopping the engine, before the oil
drains back from the cooler etc. In such cases it is
helpful to establish what the cold oil level should
be, so that it can be checked at the logical time –
before starting the engine. This can be done quite
easily by making sure that the hot oil level is correct on stopping the engine, letting it stand for
several hours and then putting an additional mark
on the dipstick. Be careful not to overfill, which is
likely to cause overheating and damage. Never remove the dipstick with the engine running since
hot oil can cause nasty burns.

(3) In normal circumstances gearbox oil does
not need changing as often as engine oil, but should
be changed at the intervals given in the handbook
or if the gearbox overheats. This might happen if,
for example, there has been a failure of engine

circulating water, apart from any overheating experienced due to clutch slip. If a filter is fitted for the gearbox oil this should be changed at the same time. When changing oil examine what is removed for any discoloration due to water, or for any metal particles – obviously an ominous sign.

(4) Periodically inspect the outside of the gearbox. A breather is usually fitted at the top and this needs to be kept clean. Check for any sign of leakage at the oil seal at the rear of the gearbox. This may be caused by a badly aligned shaft, and is most likely to be revealed by a spatter of oil thrown off by the rotating shaft.

(5) Gearbox oil coolers and their connections need similar attention as the rest of the engine cooling system – pipes to be checked and properly clipped. About every three years, depending on the waters in which the boat operates, the heat exchanger will need to be flushed through.

(6) The controls need to be checked at least every year, or whenever any work is done on the gearbox itself. The movement of the shift lever on the gearbox must exactly follow the helmsman's lever, and it should be possible to identify the engagement of ahead, neutral and astern quite positively. Badly adjusted controls are a common cause of expensive gearbox problems. With single-lever controls it is important that the throttle reduces engine rpm to idling speed before shifting gear.

(7) Careless operation can easily cause unnecessary wear. Even with single-lever controls the engine must never be put from ahead to astern, or vice versa, without dwelling in neutral long enough to let the engine slow down to tickover. Where separate gear shift and throttle levers are fitted even greater care is needed.

(8) While under way take note of any unusual sounds or vibration that might indicate gearbox wear, shaft misalignment, or propeller damage.

(9) Read the instruction book carefully in respect of your own gearbox. Some boxes have restrictions on trailing a shaft (say with twin-screw installations, or when motor sailing) so that it is necessary either to lock the shaft or to start the engine occasionally in order to circulate the gearbox oil. Less common, but still found occasionally,

are restrictions on prolonged running astern. Some gearboxes have a lock-up facility, so that they can be locked into ahead gear as a get-you-home measure in the event of hydraulic failure.

SHAFTING

Good alignment of the engine and gearbox with the shaft is essential, whether flexible couplings are fitted or not. Fig 3 shows the method of checking coupling alignment to ensure that the two parts are in line and parallel.

With the coupling bolts removed, the two halves of the coupling are rotated together, stopping every 90° to measure the gap between the two flanges with feeler gauges at the top, bottom, and on each side. Ideally, the flanges should butt together perfectly, with no measurable gap. If the misalignment is greater than one thousandth of an inch for every inch of flange diameter (that is to say 0.008in on an 8in flange), it must be adjusted at the engine

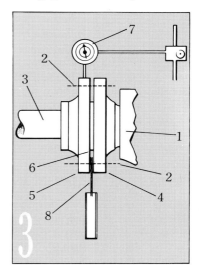

Fig 3. Checking shaft alignment: (1) gearbox; (2) coupling bolts removed; (3) propeller shaft; (4) gearbox output flange; (5) propeller shaft coupling flange; (6) spigot; (7) clock gauge mounted on gearbox, to establish concentricity of couplings; (8) feeler gauge to check alignment.

mountings – if necessary by adding or removing shims. When satisfactory alignment is obtained the engine holding down bolts must be retightened, and the alignment finally checked again.

The hull of a boat always changes shape when it is lifted from the water, so shaft alignment must always be done afloat. It is good practice to remove the coupling bolts before a boat is brought ashore and to check the alignment before reconnecting when she is put back in the water. The security of shaft coupling bolts should be examined from time to time.

PROPELLERS

The last link in the transmission chain is the propeller which has to convert the torque in the shaft into thrust to drive the boat. It is also the most vulnerable part of the whole engine installation. Fish floats and lobster pots make effective traps for the unwary, quite apart from the bits of line and plastic sheeting which swill around at sea.

When a rope gets round the screw it is likely to take several turns before it is noticed, and often it will be no easy task to unravel them. Whenever somebody is working on or near the propeller or shafting make quite certain that the engine cannot be started. If you can get hold of the end of the rope try putting the gearbox in neutral and pulling, while somebody else turns the shaft astern by hand.

If this approach fails a good job can sometimes be done with a sharp, serrated breadknife securely lashed to the end of a boat hook, but it is usually necessary to get into the water. So it is wise to carry a wet suit and face mask – and proper sub-aqua gear is even better.

Propeller design is a specialised subject, and the correct choice for a particular boat is most important if good performance is to be achieved.

Diameter, pitch (the theoretical distance the screw would move through the water in one revolution if it didn't slip), blade area and shape all have to be considered – depending on the designed speed of the boat, engine horsepower, propeller rpm, the general shape of the hull and the available

space under the stern. Diameter and pitch should usually be selected so that at full throttle the engine is running at just below its maximum rpm. With too much pitch the engine cannot develop full speed, while with too little pitch it will run too fast.

Propeller efficiency is seldom more than 60 per cent, and often below 50 per cent. Sailing craft, with low-powered engines, are often fitted with two-bladed propellers so that they can be set vertically in the aperture when under sail to reduce drag. This arrangement has the disadvantage that vibration is caused each time the blades rotate past the aperture, so where drag is not an important consideration it is better to fit a three-blader.

In any case, to reduce blade loading, more powerful engines require three or more blades. Overloading leads to cavitation due to the sudden collapse of air bubbles on the leading face of the blade, resulting in noise, loss of power and damage – which looks rather like corrosion – on the blade surface.

Propeller damage needs to be rectified as soon as possible since any out of balance forces will cause vibration and excessive wear to the bearings and sterngland. Minor nicks can be dressed up with a file but more substantial damage requires replacement of the propeller – which can be done underwater with sub-aqua gear. Specialists can repair damaged propellers at less cost than buying new.

Variable pitch propellers have a place in some specialist boats, such as those used for towing, and in motor sailers. An ordinary propeller is designed to satisfy one set of conditions – normally for maximum boat speed at the maximum power and rpm of the engine. However, if a boat is towing, full power is required at a much reduced boat speed. This calls for a lower pitch (finer) propeller than would otherwise be the case. Conversely, when motor sailing, maximum hull speed may be achieved with only low power and modest engine rpm, conditions which demand coarser pitch.

An extension of this principle is the controllable pitch propeller where the blades can be twisted round to give astern power or feathered into a neutral position, eliminating the need for a forward/reverse gearbox. In the simplest type, movement of the shaft fore and aft (in and out) controls the pitch. A somewhat bulky propeller boss is needed to accommodate the mechanism, so efficiency suffers, and it is exposed to silt and marine growth. Care is needed to prevent the engine being overloaded with too coarse a pitch, or being allowed to overspeed if the pitch is too fine.

Another form of propeller, only found in sailing craft, has hinged blades which fold together to minimise drag when under sail. When the shaft rotates centrifugal force opens up the blades and they are held open by the thrust they exert on the water. Astern power is minimal. When ordering a new or spare propeller it is important to understand the convention regarding rotation. A right-handed propeller is one which, when running

ahead, rotates in a clockwise direction as viewed from aft. In twin-screw installations the propellers should be of opposite hands, and normally outward-turning – that is to say right-handed on the starboard side and left-handed on the port. This arrangement gives good manoeuvrability at the expense of a scarcely-perceptible loss of efficiency. This counter-rotation is usually arranged in one of the gearboxes, with both engines turning in the same direction.

A propeller is normally secured by a key, as shown in Fig 4, on the tapered end of the propeller shaft, and is held in place by the propeller nut which is itself secured with some form of locking device – a lock nut, tab washer, or split pin. There may be a conical fairing over this.

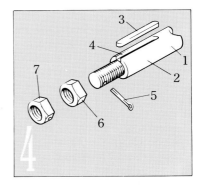

Fig 4. Propeller attachment: (1) shaft; (2) tapered portion of shaft; (3) key; (4) keyway; (5) split pin for lock nut; (6) propeller nut; (7) lock nut.

When driving ahead the propeller forces itself onto the tapered shaft, where it is inclined to bind quite hard, sometimes making subsequent removal very difficult. Most boatyards and marine engineers have special extractors for this purpose, but otherwise a few good blows with a heavy hammer on the propeller boss will often do the trick – having first unscrewed the propeller nut two or three turns and cushioned the boss against the hammer with a block of wood. Be careful not to damage the blades, and when the propeller is removed do not lose the key.

OUTDRIVES

Outdrive units (see Fig 5) – also known as stern-drives or inboard/outboards – and saildrive units are becoming increasingly popular methods of converting power into thrust.

Outdrives are available for a wide range of powers and incorporate several useful features. They are popular with boatbuilders because they are easy to fit, with no alignment problems. The component parts are engineered so that the whole drive line is correctly matched. Designers like them because the engine is situated right aft where it does not intrude into the accommodation in terms of space or noise.

And boat owners like them because they make the boat very manoeuvrable at high speeds, and because the unit includes a universal joint which allows the propeller to be swivelled for steering and to be raised. This serves two purposes. Trimming the unit in or out a little raises or lowers the bow of the boat to achieve optimum trim – while getting the boat 'over the hump' and onto the plane, for example, or to suit particular sea conditions and loading. The tilt mechanism can also be used to raise the propeller almost clear of the water, either for attention or when the boat is to be trailed. Some form of lock is incorporated so that the leg is kept 'down' when the gear is put astern.

From the universal joint the drive passes to bevel gears (which usually incorporate the ahead/neutral/astern mechanism) at the top of the vertical drive shaft, and then to another set of bevel gears at the bottom of the unit to drive the propeller. The great majority of outdrives are steerable, so that the entire unit can be swung around the vertical axis to direct the propeller thrust in whichever direction is required – either ahead or astern.

Transmitting the drive through two sets of bevel gears does result in some loss of efficiency, and there is also the drag of the underwater unit to consider. It also has to be said that the outdrive is more vulnerable to damage and corrosion than a conventional inboard installation. On the plus side the propeller is more accessible in the event of accidental fouling.

Correct maintenance is important in accordance with the maker's instructions. These are likely to include regular attention to check the oil level and detect water, which may get access through defective seals or via the large rubber gaiter which surrounds the universal joint for the trim/tilt mechanism. Some makers recommend that this rubber gaiter is replaced every season.

The body of the underwater unit is made of aluminium alloy, so it is particularly important to preserve paint surfaces (always using the recommended paint), and to replace the sacrificial zinc anodes when required. Grease nipples need attention as directed in the handbook, and the hoses which connect cooling water and exhaust to the engine should be checked regularly. The cooling-water inlet, fitted near the forward side of the underwater unit, must be kept clean.

Boats fitted with outdrives (or with outboard engines) have quite different handling characteristics compared to those with conventional propellers and rudders. It must be remembered that there is no effective steering unless the propeller is rotating either ahead or astern. When manoeuvring, first angle the propeller in the required direction before engaging ahead or astern gear as the case may be.

THE VOLVO PENTA DUOPROP DRIVE

In 1983 Volvo Penta introduced Duoprop, two contra-rotating propellers on a single outdrive leg from an inboard diesel. Duoprop gave petrol engine performance to diesels and in 1986 it was made available for petrol units as well.

One propeller creates a paddle wheel effect. But when two props on a single drive are set to rotate in opposite directions they produce transverse forces which counterbalance one another. Duoprop's twin props double the blade area, thereby halving the power required. And that means half the load, half the tip and induced losses, and lower cavitation. This cuts down on vibration and noise. Furthermore, the axially symmetrical water jet created meanss that every bit of energy is used to produce forward thrust. Greater efficiency means less fuel.

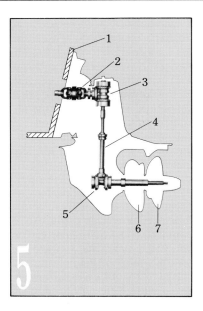

Fig 5. The principle of the Volvo Penta Duoprop drive: (1) boat's transom; (2) universal joint allowing outdrive leg to be swivelled and raised; (3) ahead/neutral/astern gears, with cone clutches; (4) vertical drive shaft; (5) two bevel gears, driving the two propellers in opposite directions; (6) conventional forward propeller; (7) semi-cavitating aft propeller.

In terms of manoeuvrability, the contra-rotating prop system provides straight steering whether the boat is on or off the plane and reduces any tendency to roll on the hull. At high speed the props take a grip on the water and in rougher seas keep the boat up on the plane. Tests have shown improved acceleration of more than 30 per cent compared with single props, plus consistently higher top speeds.

SAILDRIVES

Saildrives are similar in principle to outdrives except that they are fitted through a hole in the bottom of the boat instead of through the transom, and as the leg is fixed with no arrangement for steering or tilting, they are mechanically simpler. The general layout is shown in Fig 6. To maintain the boat's watertight integrity it is essential that the rubber seal where the unit passes through the hull is kept in good condition. This requires renewal at intervals of not more than five years or according to the maker's instructions. When fitted in sailing yachts these units often have folding propellers.

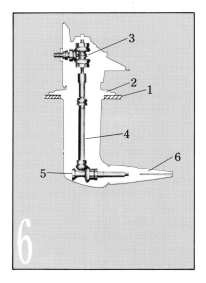

Fig 6. Saildrive installation: (1) bottom of boat; (2) rubber seal; (3) ahead/neutral/astern gears; (4) vertical drive shaft; (5) bevel gear to final drive; (6) folding propeller.

8. ELECTRICS

Batteries – Charging equipment – Split charging systems –
Other battery chargers – Electric starters – Non-electric starters –
Starting aids

While a few small engines can be started by hand, almost all boat engines have electric starters. Quite apart from this, electricity is used to power an ever-increasing range of auxiliary and domestic equipment. Ashore, we tend to take electricity for granted, but a boat has to generate and store her own power – and marine electrical systems are probably the most vulnerable and delicate parts of any engine installation.

Marine standards demand special materials and effective paint systems to resist corrosion, adequate sealing and careful insulation to guard against short circuits and current leakage, and good ventilation to combat high temperatures which occur in boats' engine spaces.

Of course, there has to be adequate battery capacity to cope with the demand imposed on the system, with some spare capacity to allow for later additions and ageing batteries. Except in the smallest boats, separate batteries should be fitted for engine starting and auxiliary purposes.

Because most boats operate on a relatively low voltage – 12V, or 24V in some larger craft – the currents involved are fairly high, so cable runs have to be of adequate cross-section, properly supported. Diesel engines make heavy demands on their starting batteries: several hundred amperes are needed to get a cold engine into life. Special cables and batteries are available to cope with this.

Steps have to be taken to suppress the interference caused by electrical equipment to radio and other navigational aids. And finally, this complicated system has to be operated correctly and sensibly, so switches and control boards must be conveniently sited, and all cables colour-coded and labelled.

BATTERIES

Most boats have lead-acid batteries, similar to those used in cars or lorries, although there is a more expensive alternative in the form of alkaline (nickel-cadmium) batteries which have a longer life and need less maintenance.

The capacity of a battery is given in ampere hours, normally assuming that the discharge takes place over a period of ten hours – a ten-hour rating. For example, a 200-amp-hour battery will supply 20 amps for 10 hours. But if the discharge is at a higher rate – say over five hours – its capacity will be reduced to something like 150 amp hours.

No battery will give out quite as much electricity as you put in. Its efficiency depends on design and age, but a typical charge/discharge ratio is about 1.4:1, so a charge of 140 amp hours is needed to restore a discharge of 100 amp hours.

Even when not in use, a lead-acid battery slowly discharges (more quickly in warm conditions), so it will have to be recharged every month or so. Allowing a battery to discharge completely, whether by use or by standing idle, and then recharging it is known as 'deep cycling'. This is harmful to the plates inside the battery and reduces its life. The number of times a battery will tolerate deep cycling depends upon its design and type – special *traction* batteries are available, if necessary.

The state of charge of a battery is indicated by the specific gravity of the electrolyte, using a hydrometer. At 60°F (16°C) 1.260–1.280 for a lead-acid battery indicates that it is fully charged, 1.190–1.210 half discharged, and 1.110–1.130 fully discharged. The condition of a battery (as opposed to

HOW AN ALTERNATOR WORKS

All generators depend on the inter-relationship between magnetism and electricity. It is well known that if you wind a length of wire around an iron core, such as a nail, and pass an electric current through the wire, the iron will become magnetised. Conversely, if you move a wire through a magnetic field, a current will be *induced* in the wire.

An alternator makes use of both of these principles: a small electric current is passed through coils of thin wire – the *field windings* – on a central rotor. This creates a magnetic field, which, when the rotor spins, cuts across a mass of windings – the *stator* – to create an electric current.

Because the stator is subjected to an ever-changing magnetic field, first from a north pole then from a south pole, the current flow repeatedly reverses direction (AC).

The voltage produced depends both on the speed at which the rotor is turning and the current passing through the field windings. The speed, of course, depends on the speed at which the engine is running, but the voltage can still be controlled by adjusting the current in the field coils. That is the job of the *regulator*. The *rectifier* converts the AC produced by the stator coils into DC by means of a series of diodes, serving as one-way valves.

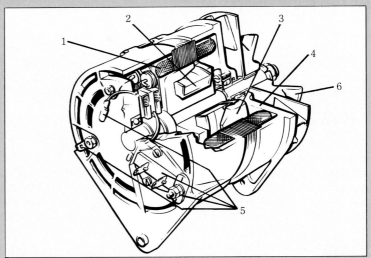

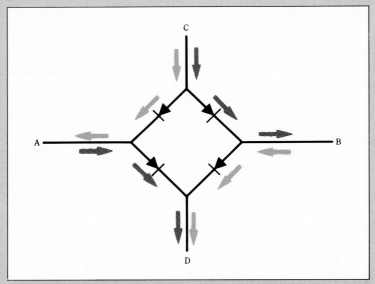

Top: an alternator: (1) stator coils; (2) field coils; (3) rotor; (4) housing; (5) rectifier and regulator; connections and (6) drive pulley. Above: a simplified rectifier – the diodes allow current to flow only in the direction of the arrows, thus converting AC in wires A and B to DC in wires C and D.

its state of charge) can be found with a special tester applied to each 2V cell in turn, when the battery is at least 70 per cent fully charged. A healthy cell should maintain a steady voltage for ten seconds. Over a period of time the water contained in the electrolyte (acid) of a lead-acid battery tends to evaporate, so replace it by topping up with distilled water so that the level of the electrolyte is kept just above the lead plates. Some modern versions of lead-acid batteries are sealed, eliminating the need to top up the electrolyte, and minimising the amount of hydrogen released when charging, thus reducing the possibility of an explosion.

Despite the 'maintenance-free' tag applied to such batteries, the fact remains that no battery is completely maintenance free: at the very least they must all be kept dry and clean, with their connections tight and lightly smeared with petroleum jelly. They need good ventilation, and must be firmly secured and mounted in an acid-proof tray.

CHARGING EQUIPMENT

Nearly all modern engines are fitted with alternators producing alternating current (AC). Unfortunately, batteries can only store direct current (DC), so the AC supply from the alternator is converted into DC by a built-in rectifier (see diagram).

Older engines were fitted with dynamos, which produced DC directly, but they had more moving parts and therefore proved less reliable. Moreover, an alternator has a bigger output that a DC generator of the same size and can operate over a wide range of speed so that (with a suitable pulley drive ratio) reasonable output is provided even at low engine speeds (see Fig 1). Alternators are, however, more liable to electrical damage than dynamos. If, for example, the battery is switched off or disconnected while the alternator is charging, damage may be caused to the regulator and the rectifying diodes. This can be prevented by incorporating a switch which de-energises the alternator field coils before the battery switch can be opened. Also the regulator and diodes are likely to be damaged if the battery is connected the wrong way round, or if the system is tested using a 'Megger' type instrument,

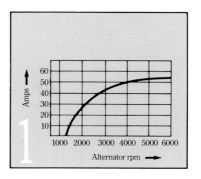

Fig 1. Typical output of a marine alternator at ambient temperature of 77°F (25°C) – cutting-in speed 1150rpm and maximum speed 10,000rpm.

or even by using an arc welder on board while the alternator is connected.

Obviously the alternator must have enough capacity to recharge the batteries within the expected running time of the engine, while at the same time supplying the electrical power required to run the boat's systems. Unless you have recently added so much electrical equipment that the alternator is now too small for the system, the most likely reason for it failing to function is a slack drive belt: so the belt tension should be checked regularly, and adjusted if necessary. It should not be possible to deflect it more than ½in (12mm) when depressed in the middle of its longest run. Carry a spare. Every four years or so the alternator should be sent to an auto-electrical specialist for servicing.

The charging circuit (see Fig 2) should incorporate a voltmeter. With the engine running, this shows the voltage supplied by the alternator to the battery, and when the engine is stopped, it shows the present voltage of the battery (but does not tell you how long this will be available). There should also be an ammeter to show how much current the alternator is delivering to the battery. From these two instruments you can get some idea of what is happening. For example, after a period of rest, the general service battery voltage is likely to have dropped due to the use of lights etc, while the starting battery should still be well up. When the engine

Fig 2. Simplified electrical circuit:
(1) battery (note heavy leads to
starter); (2) alternator; (3) regulator
(shown separate for illustrative
purposes, but normally integral with
alternator); (4) starter motor; (5)
starter relay; (6) heater/starter
switch; (7) fuse; (8) fast fuse to
protect alternator from reverse
polarity; (9) warning lamp; (10)
ammeter; (11) starting aid; (12)
voltmeter, with switch.

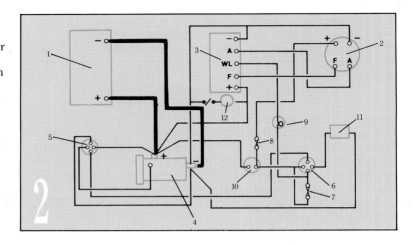

is started the recharging current will be relatively high, gradually reducing as charge is restored.

A red warning lamp is usually included in the alternator field circuit, which lights when the engine switch is first made on starting to show that the battery is supplying current to the alternator field windings. When the engine starts and the alternator begins to charge the lamp goes out. If it fails to show when switching on, it may indicate that the battery is flat (or not connected), or that the alternator or regulator is faulty, or the starting switch has failed, or there is a bad connection somewhere. Or it might just mean that the bulb has failed! If the light doesn't go out once the engine is running, check the alternator drive belt, but otherwise it points to some discontinuity in the circuit or a faulty alternator or regulator.

SPLIT CHARGING SYSTEMS

Where separate engine starting and general service batteries are fitted, there are various ways that charging can be arranged. The simplest arrangement, at least on a twin-engined boat, is to have two completely separate charging systems, one battery being charged by each engine, but with a *parallelling switch* so that the two sets of batteries can be connected together for engine starting.

A more complex system is called for if starting and service batteries are both to be charged from one alternator. Just connecting them all up together would result in one battery discharging into the other, possibly leaving both batteries too flat to be of any use. Depending on whether the alternator is battery-sensed or machine-sensed, this calls either for *blocking diodes* (which allow current to flow in one direction only, see Fig 3) or for an *electro-mechanical relay*. With a machine-sensed alternator, the voltage is controlled by a regulator connected to the output terminals of the alternator. This limits the output voltage of the alternator to a level too low to compensate for the inevitable drop in voltage across a blocking diode, so a split charge relay is essential.

A battery-sensed alternator monitors the voltage at the battery terminals, so the more reliable blocking diode can be employed, as the alternator output voltage will automatically rise to compensate for any voltage drop in the system and give an effective charging voltage at the battery of 14.2V (for a 12V system) or 28.4V (for a 24V system).

OTHER BATTERY CHARGERS

Diesels thrive on work – low power operation causes poor combustion and consequent deposits within the engine. So almost nothing is worse for a diesel engine than prolonged running out of gear

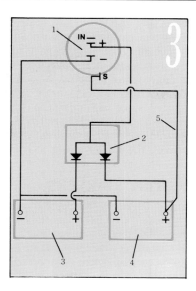

Fig 3. The use of blocking diodes for charging two batteries from one alternator: (1) alternator; (2) blocking diodes, permitting current flow in direction of arrow heads only; (3) engine starting battery; (4) general services battery; (5) sensing lead.

generator built into a sound-proofed box in the engineroom, and fitted with remote start and stop controls near the galley. As well as supplying 240V AC for galley equipment and the battery charger, it may also supply a converter to provide 12 or 24V DC to reduce the drain on the batteries.

Where shore power is not available, solar panels provide a useful alternative. They do not require bright sunlight, but their output is obviously greater in summer because of the longer hours of daylight. Panels incorporate a blocking diode to prevent the battery discharging whenever the operating voltage is not reached.

Wind generators are popular in some areas where there is enough wind to provide the essential power. However, they are rather noisy.

For serious ocean-going vessels that are powered by sail there are two other possibilities. One is a shaft generator, driven from the trailing propeller shaft, which can produce about 12 amps. The other is a generator driven by a spinner, towed astern.

ELECTRIC STARTERS

Engine-starter batteries should be kept in good condition, because if their voltage is too low the starter will only turn the engine over slowly. This reduces the likelihood of a successful start and causes an excessive current to flow through the starter which could damage it.

For much the same reason, the cables between the battery and the starter motor need to be heavy enough and as short as possible to minimise the voltage drop, and their connections kept clean and tight. In order to achieve this, the main electrical circuit to the starter motor does not run through the starter switch at the helmsman's position. Instead the 'starter switch' serves as a remote control, operating a solenoid or starter relay which actually makes the connection between the battery and starter.

There are two main types of starter. An inertia starter has its pinion (gear) mounted on a long shaft along which runs a spiral groove. When the starter motor first starts to turn, the inertia of the pinion prevents it from turning – so instead it winds

just to charge the batteries. If batteries cannot be kept properly charged by the normal operation of the boat's machinery, other arrangements must be made to keep the batteries in good shape.

For boats kept in marinas where shore power is available, a marine battery charger is the obvious solution. A purpose-made marine charger automatically adjusts the charging rate as the battery becomes fully charged, preventing the overcharging which will occur if a car battery trickle charger is used. At the same time, some versions are able to supply a limited amount of power to run equipment aboard, though not all are able to cope with split charging systems.

In larger craft, an auxiliary generator is a worthwhile alternative or back-up to shore supplies, and it is essential if your power demand is likely to be more than the 5 amps or so of 240V AC which seems to be the most many marinas can supply. A typical installation comprises an engine-driven itself along the shaft, to engage with the ring gear. When the engine fires and the starter switch is released the reverse happens, and the still-spinning pinion winds itself back along the now-stationary shaft. To prevent sluggish operation and the failure of the pinion to engage or disengage properly, the gear needs to be kept clean and requires occasional lubrication with a light oil.

Pre-engaged starters are more commonly fitted to diesel engines. In this case the first action of the solenoid is to engage the pinion with the flywheel: only then is contact made to actuate the starter motor itself. This has the advantage of reducing wear on the pinion and on the flywheel teeth, and reduces the possibility of the pinion being disengaged prematurely when the engine first fires.

If operating the starter switch produces a clicking sound from the starter but no rotation, the first thing to check is the state of the battery. Assuming this is well-charged and the connections are all clean and tight, the chances are that the starter itself is faulty.

A click and a whirring sound indicates that the pinion has failed to engage although the starter is operating correctly. This can sometimes be rectified by tapping the starter motor with a mallet, but a better and more lasting cure is to remove the starter motor and clean the spiral groove in the pinion shaft.

Total silence may show that the battery is flat, or that there is trouble with the solenoid or with the circuit to it from the starter switch.

It should be possible to locate the defect by systematic checking of the circuitry. The solenoid has two pairs of cables running to it. The smaller pair of cables run to and from the starter switch at the helmsman's position. If these are carefully shorted out (or jumped) with a screwdriver and the starter then functions, there is a defect in the control circuit to and from the starter switch, and there is no problem with the solenoid or the starter itself.

As a last resort, with an inertia starter, it is possible to jump the two main terminals so that the solenoid is eliminated. Beware that a heavy current will flow and sparks will fly, so that this and similar procedures must never be followed when there is any risk at all of explosive vapour being present and certainly not with a petrol engine. If the starter then functions it points to a defective solenoid, and it is advisable to carry a spare. This approach of jumping the solenoid does not help to get the engine started with a pre-engaged starter since although the starter may rotate it will not engage with the flywheel. However, it should help to establish whether the trouble lies with the starter motor or the solenoid.

NON-ELECTRIC STARTERS

Apart from hand starting, a variety of non-electric starting methods have been developed over the years, with varying degrees of success.

Hydraulic starters use oil, pressurised in an accumulator charged with compressed gas, to operate a hydraulic motor fitted in place of the electric starter. A pump, driven by the engine once it is running, recharges the accumulator, while a hand pump is available for the initial charge.

Spring starters can be used either as a main starter or as an emergency unit. A spring, compressed by winding a handle by hand, is released by flicking a switch, and drives a pinion exactly like an inertia electric starter. They are suitable for diesels of up to 6 litres, and, being entirely manually operated, are inherently reliable.

STARTING AIDS

Petrol engines are invariably fitted with a choke or strangler in the air inlet which provides a richer mixture for starting. If the choke is left closed ('out') for too long the engine will stop due to the mixture being too rich and the plugs getting wet with fuel. Many manufacturers now overcome this by fitting automatic chokes.

Diesel engines sometimes experience problems starting from cold because so much of the heat from compression is lost into the cold surfaces around the cylinder and the incoming air is not heated sufficiently to ignite the fuel.

A variety of methods are used to overcome this, one such being the excess fuel device mentioned in

Fig 4. Thermostart starting aid: (1) fuel inlet; (2) tubular body; (3) terminals; (4) heater coil; (5) igniter; (6) igniter shield; (7) insulating bush; (8) needle valve stem; (9) ball valve.

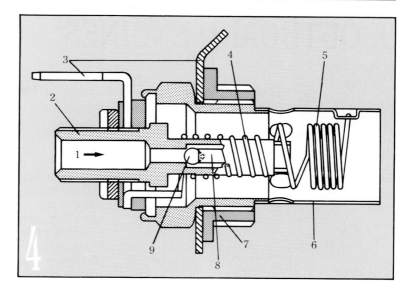

chapter 4. In some small engines, particularly those intended for hand starting, a decompressor is fitted to increase the cranking speed. This consists of a lever on top of the cylinder head which holds the exhaust valves off their seats. When the engine is rotating as fast as possible the lever is released to restore compression. It must not be used for stopping the engine.

A fairly common starting aid for diesel engines is an electric heater (or glow) plug in each combustion space. These are switched on for about 20 seconds before the starter is operated. The correct operation of heater plugs can be checked visually by removing them from the engine and inspecting them: they should literally glow.

Another form of internal heater is the Lucas Thermostart unit (see Fig 4) fitted to the air intakes for starting in temperatures down to 0°F (−18°C). Switching on the Thermostart energises a heater coil, and, by thermal expansion, opens a ball valve. This releases a small quantity of diesel fuel from an integral reservoir to an electric igniter, and the burning fuel warms the air in the inlet manifold.

A few engines employ a controlled injection of ether into the inlet manifold. This is effective for low temperatures and for engines with a high compression ratio, but the operative word is 'controlled': the indiscriminate use of aerosol canisters of ether can damage the engine, because the liquid is so volatile that it tends to explode while the piston is still on its compression stroke. If, as a last resort, a hand-held aerosol is used, use it very sparingly.

A small number of engines have little oil cups on the inlet manifold. These are filled from an oil can before starting, when the oil is drawn into the cylinders to improve the seal between the piston rings and the cylinder walls and raise the compression. The same effect can be achieved by removing the air filter and squirting a small amount of oil into the air inlet as the engine is cranked.

9. OUTBOARD ENGINES

The two-stroke cycle – Two-stroke fuel and oil – Starting – Ignition – Cooling – The lower unit – Installation – Running in – Routine maintenance – A submerged engine

An outboard motor can be a very attractive power unit for a small boat, and is the only realistic en-gine for a dinghy. Outboards are easy to fit, do not occupy space within the hull, have a good power/weight ratio, and – in the smaller sizes at least – are easily portable for servicing and storage.

Their main disadvantage is high running costs: most consume fairly large quantities of petrol for the power they produce; and spares, although widely available, tend to be expensive. Secondary drawbacks, perhaps, but of increasing significance are the high noise levels associated with outboard engine installations, and the high proportions of hydrocarbons, carbon monoxide and nitrogen oxides in their exhausts.

Almost all these characteristics stem from the fact that the vast majority of outboards are two-stroke petrol engines, though there are a few four-stroke petrol units, and a growing interest in diesels.

One feature common to all outboards is that the crankshaft is mounted vertically. At the top is the flywheel, together with the starting gear and the ignition system, while the other end of the crank-shaft is connected to a long vertical shaft running inside the immersed leg of the outboard. This terminates in a bevel gear, which drives the hori-zontal propeller shaft.

The leg also includes the circulating water pump for engine cooling, the exhaust pipe, and – on all but the smallest engines – the ahead/neutral/astern gears.

On bigger outboards, the propeller drive is usu-ally taken through a splined rubber hub, which protects the gears and the rest of the engine by allowing the drive to slip if the propeller hits any-thing solid. Smaller engines achieve the same effect

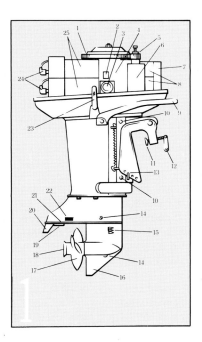

Fig 1. Two-cylinder outboard: (1) flywheel; (2) fuel filter; (3) fuel pump; (4) crankcase; (5) starter pinion; (6) starter; (7) air silencer; (8) carburettors; (9) carrying handle; (10) swivel brackets; (11) transom clamps; (12) locking holes; (13) tilt adjustment; (14) gearcase oil plugs; (15) cooling-water inlet; (16) skeg; (17) propeller; (18) exhaust through hub; (19) anode; (20) trim tab; (21) cavitation plate; (22) cooling-water outlet; (23) gear shift; (24) spark plugs; (25) cylinders.

Fig 2. In a two-stroke engine the sealed crankcase plays an important part in the transfer of fuel and air into the combustion chamber.

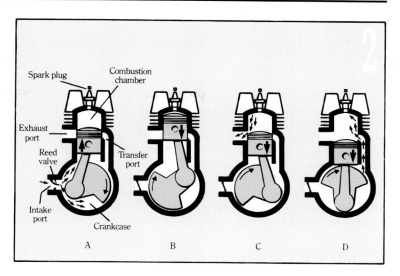

by means of either a shear pin or a spring drive. The shear pin is designed to break if it is overloaded, so it is essential to carry a spare. Spring drives will stand several such shocks, but even so it is worth carrying a spare, as metal fatigue can cause sudden failure.

An outboard-powered boat doesn't need a rudder, as steering is achieved by swinging the engine around a vertical axis to vary the direction of the propeller thrust. This requires a special handling technique, because there is little or no steering effect when the propeller is not turning.

The smallest engines have no astern gear, but pivot through 360° to give astern power. And some of the very simplest do not have a 'neutral' or de-clutch facility – so make sure that the boat is pointing in a safe direction before starting up.

All outboards can be tilted, to raise their propellers when approaching shallow water. Tilting the engine further lifts the prop clear of the water altogether when it is out of use.

THE TWO-STROKE CYCLE

A two-stroke engine combines induction, compression, power and exhaust into one revolution of the crankshaft or two strokes of the piston. There are

no inlet or exhaust valves: instead the flow of fuel/air mixture is controlled by the movement of the piston itself (see Fig 2).

As the piston rises (A) fuel/air mixture is drawn from the carburettor, through the reed (non-return) valve, into the sealed crankcase. At this stage, the transfer and exhaust ports are blocked by the piston, so the previous charge, already in the combustion chamber, is compressed.

As the piston approaches the top of its stroke, the compressed mixture is ignited, driving the piston down on its working stroke (B). The downward movement of the piston builds up pressure within the crankcase.

Towards the bottom of its stroke (C) the piston uncovers the exhaust port, letting the burnt exhaust gas out of the cylinder. Shortly afterwards, it uncovers the transfer port, allowing the new charge to flow into the cylinder from the crankcase.

The incoming charge helps push the exhaust gases out of the cylinder – a process known as *scavenging*. Early two-strokes were *cross-scavenged*, with the transfer port opposite the exhaust port. To avoid the incoming charge going straight across the cylinder and out the other side, the piston crown had a deflector to direct the new charge upwards.

But this required a very long, narrow combustion chamber. Higher engine speeds can be achieved by engines with short, wide combustion chambers, so most modern engines are *loop-scavenged*. Each cylinder has a pair of transfer ports, on the same side of the cylinder as the exhaust port, so the new charge 'loops' around the combustion chamber to drive out the exhaust gases.

No matter how carefully the engine has been designed and built, it is impossible to prevent some mixing of the new charge with the exhaust. This affects efficiency, hence two-strokes' thirst for fuel. But it is also the key to the two-stroke's ability to produce a power stroke on every revolution of the crankshaft, hence their high power/weight ratio.

TWO-STROKE FUEL AND OIL

As the crankcase of a two-stroke acts as a pump, pushing fuel/air mixture into the cylinder, it follows that each part of the crankcase has to be separate and sealed from the next. Nor can there be a conventional oil sump in the bottom of the crankcase. Instead, oil is mixed with the fuel, in proportions ranging from 1:10 to 1:100 depending on the engine. Obviously it is important to get the proportions right.

The warmth in the crankcase vaporises the fuel, leaving most of the oil as a film on the working surfaces, with some being carried into the combustion chamber to lubricate the piston rings and cylinder bore.

Two-stroke outboard oil needs special properties, and is quite different to four-stroke oil. It must mix readily and permanently with petrol, and requires additives to reduce carbon deposits in the combustion chamber and on the spark plugs. Other additives resist the effects of acidic products of combustion and protect the engine from corrosion.

Always use the oil specified for the engine: usually this will be one which meets the test procedure of the American Boating Industry Association, marked BIA TC-W – the last three letters meaning 'two-cycle, water-cooled'.

Until recently, the oil was mixed with the petrol in the correct proportions before putting it in the fuel tank. Where it is necessary to mix petrol and oil this should be done accurately and carefully, but many new outboards have a small separate tank for lubricating oil. The oil is then automatically mixed with the fuel in a pump operated by crankcase pressure and vacuum pulses. This injects the right amount of oil depending on the power setting, varying the fuel/oil ratio from, for example, 100:1 at idling speed to 50:1 at full throttle.

Although it is advisable to check with the engine handbook, nearly all outboards will run on leaded or unleaded fuel.

Small outboards have integral fuel tanks mounted on top of the engine, with gravity feed to the carburettor. The filling cap incorporates an air vent and it is important to open this before starting the engine, otherwise a partial vacuum will develop inside the tank, and the engine will stop due to fuel starvation. It is just as important to remember to close the vent when the engine is not in use, in order to prevent fuel leakage when the engine is moved.

A larger outboard, one of more than about 10hp (7.5kW), is likely to have a separate portable fuel tank connected to the engine by a hose. The hose incorporates a hand bulb for priming the system, but once the engine is running its fuel pump takes over. In the event of fuel pump failure, continuous pumping with the hand bulb may ensure that you get home.

Petrol in a two-stroke is just as dangerous as in a four-stroke engine. When mixing or refuelling always do it outside the boat to avoid any spillage or petrol vapour collecting in the bilges – and of course there must be no smoking or naked lights in the vicinity. Care is also needed when transporting engines or portable fuel tanks. For small engines with integral tanks make sure that the fuel cock is turned off and that the filler cap is secure with the air vent closed. With a portable tank remove the hose both from the engine and the tank, so that any fuel is retained within the tank and is not in the hose. If an air vent is fitted see that it is closed (most tanks have automatic venting arrangements).

STARTING

Small engines have a manual (recoil) starter on top of the powerhead. Take care when working on this (perhaps to fit a new rope) since the spring can suddenly uncoil and cause injury: wear stout gloves and eye protection. Engines above about 15hp (11kW) are usually fitted with electric starters, requiring a battery, although there may also be provision for manual starting. Most recent engines have an interlock so that the starter will only operate when the gear shift is in neutral. Although this should never be disconnected or interfered with, it's one of the first things to check if there is a starting problem.

IGNITION

Although a few small engines are still made with magneto ignition systems – and a large number of all sizes are still giving good service – nearly all new outboards have *capacitor discharge* (CD) systems.

Each plug has its own coil, so there's no distributor. Magnets in the flywheel rim generate a low voltage, which is stored in a capacitor. Sensor magnets in the flywheel activate *silicon controlled rectifiers,* which select the appropriate ignition coil primary winding, to generate a high voltage for each coil in turn. The sealed unit has no moving parts and is very reliable, as well as producing a healthy spark with anything up to 50,000 volts.

This allows the use of surface gap spark plugs, where the spark jumps radially from a central electrode. These are less prone to fouling than conventional plugs, and have no gap to adjust. They should, however, be replaced when the central electrode erodes to more than 0.030in (0.80mm) below the flat end of the plug or if it gets worn to a point.

If engine trouble is experienced and the ignition is suspect, first check the plugs, wiring, and connections before considering the CD ignition system, which can only be tested and repaired with the right equipment. And if electrical components have to be removed for any reason, make sure to label all the wires so that they can be re-connected correctly.

COOLING

Apart from one or two small units all outboards are raw-water cooled – larger engines are fitted with thermostats, set to open at about 140°F (60°C). At higher engine speeds the increased water pump pressure may be used to lift a relief valve and increase the flow of circulating water. A small leak-off on the aft side of the engine gives a visual check of the water flow.

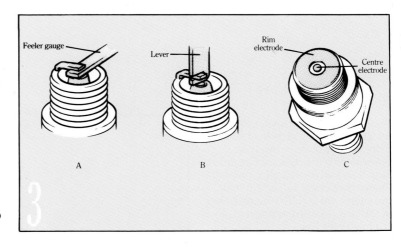

Fig 3. Spark plugs are sensitive parts of a two-stroke engine. They should be removed and cleaned after every 100 hours' running, or if misfiring occurs. Check the gap with a feeler gauge – typically it should be about 0.030in (0.80mm). If necessary the gap can be adjusted with a special lever (B), but never touch the central electrode. Modern engines with CD ignition may use surface gap plugs (C).

In the event of overheating or lack of flow, first check that the water inlet is not blocked and then check the thermostat's operation. If these two items are correct the trouble points to the water pump in the lower unit. An outboard must never be run dry, or damage will result to the water pump impeller.

When taking an engine off a boat always stand it vertically for a while until all the water has drained out, and when laying it down keep the powerhead above the lower unit to prevent any possibility of water getting in through the exhaust ports. An outboard should always be stored vertically resting on its normal supports and not on the skeg.

THE LOWER UNIT

Being underwater all its working life, the lower unit is a vulnerable part of the engine. The gearcase is filled with a special gear oil, and the handbook should give the specification together with the capacity. Typically the oil should be changed after the first 20 hours, and then checked after every 50 hours running. Drain and refill every 100 hours or at least once a season.

To do this, run the engine to warm up the oil, stand it upright and remove first the upper (level/vent) plug and then the lower (fill/drain) plug. Check the oil for water, which gives it a milky look;

and for overheating which gives it a black colour and a distinctive burnt smell. Squirt in the new oil from its plastic container through the lower plug until it appears at the upper plug. Replace the upper plug and then the lower one, using new seals if required.

Any chips or scratches in the protective paint system should be made good as soon as possible. A zinc anode is normally fitted and this should be examined regularly and replaced when it is 30 per cent eroded. It must not be painted.

INSTALLATION

First make sure that you have the right power of engine for the boat concerned. If it is too small it will not produce the required speed, nor will it have any reserve power for unforeseen circumstances such as a dirty bottom, a strong head wind or a choppy sea. On the other hand, too powerful an engine will be heavy at the stern of the boat, unduly expensive, and possibly even dangerous to operate. Furthermore too large an engine will have to run at low rpm for ordinary cruising, and with a two-stroke, this can lead to plugs oiling up, as often happens in boats operating within the speed restrictions imposed on inland waters.

Even a dinghy's small outboard must be mounted correctly for efficient performance but this is

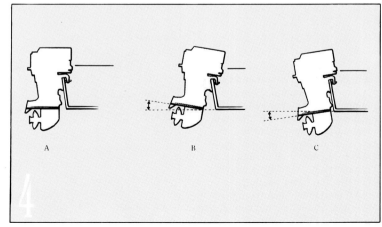

Fig 4. Correct installation, as in (A) with the cavitation plate level with the bottom of the boat, is important. Subsequently the right trim angle can be determined for optimum running. Shown here exaggerated, trimming the engine out as in (B) raises the bow of the boat, while trimming it in as in (C) lowers the bow.

more important still with larger engines. The transom height determines the required shaft length – defined as the distance from the bearing surface of the engine clamps (where they sit on the transom) to the horizontal cavitation plate above the propeller. Smaller outboards are usually available with standard shafts that are 15in (381mm) or long shafts of 20in (508mm).

Larger engines are offered either with long shafts or extra-long shafts of 25in (635mm).

The engine should be installed so that the cavitation plate is level and in line with the bottom of the boat. In heavier craft the engine can be slightly lower, and in light planing boats it can be a bit higher (to reduce underwater drag), but if put too high the cooling-water inlet may be exposed and it may cause cavitation of the propeller.

Cavitation is due to water vaporising at areas of very low pressure on the back of the propeller blade (the forward side in relation to the boat), and forming cavities which suddenly collapse when they reach higher pressure areas. This results in loss of power, particularly on high-speed turns, and in damage to the propeller. In faster planing boats there is always likely to be some cavitation, while very fast craft operate under fully cavitating conditions with most of the thrust coming from the working (aft) faces of the propeller blades.

The right propeller is needed for good performance, so outboard manufacturers offer propellers of different pitch and diameter for each of their engines depending on the intended application. Since it is easy to change the propeller of an outboard, it is quite practicable to have two different propellers for different uses of the boat. On a runabout, for example, a larger pitch might be chosen for maximum speed, but changed for a finer pitch for when the boat is more heavily loaded, as when towing a skier. Any outboard dealer will give advice on this.

Just as important as the height of the propeller is the way that it is angled (trimmed) fore and aft. With small engines the trim can be adjusted by hand in perhaps three or four positions, and once selected is normally left alone. But larger engines have power trim, whereby the leg can be trimmed in or out while running, varying the direction of the propeller thrust to trim the bow of the boat down or up to suit the conditions.

While small engines are simply clamped in place (be sure to do the clamps up really tight), those of more than about 40hp (30kW) are secured by bolts through the transom.

Even if your engine is permanently bolted to the transom, some other form of security is always required to protect it against theft – insurance companies are unlikely to pay out on an outboard which has been stolen unless it has been secured with a proprietary anti-theft device.

RUNNING IN

Having become the proud owner of an engine and fitted it to your boat, don't be in a hurry to dash away at full speed. With a new engine or one that has had a major overhaul you must follow the maker's instructions for running it in.

A typical routine would be to run at very low speed for the first 15 minutes and then slowly increase to half throttle during the next 45 minutes. For the second hour of operation gradually increase to three-quarter throttle, and then periodically increase to full throttle for a minute or two at a time. After these two hours the length of time at full throttle can be gradually extended, but full power should not be used for more than about five minutes at a time until the engine has run for at least ten hours. As it is unlikely that you'll fit the whole sequence into one day you'll find it useful to keep a record of running hours.

The fuel/oil mixture specified for the break-in period will almost certainly be lower than for normal running (perhaps 20:1 instead of 50:1). To achieve this in engines fitted with automatic oil injection it is necessary to put the recommended mixture into the tank.

Some larger engines in semi-permanent installations may be fitted with a tachometer, but otherwise it is advisable to have a suitable hand-held instrument for checking engine rpm, so that you can be certain that it is not over-speeding but that it is achieving its designed speed. Otherwise you are working in the dark.

ROUTINE MAINTENANCE

An outboard is so exposed to the elements that it is particularly important that all the lubrication points mentioned in its handbook are treated with water-resistant grease every month, or as recommended.

These include all throttle, choke and control linkages, clamp screws, pivot points, propeller shaft, cover latch and tilt lock together with the trim/tilt mechanism, steering gear and starter pinion helix where fitted. Also where appropriate the power trim/tilt reservoir needs to be checked and topped up.

Check and clean the spark plugs regularly.

Be careful that only the cleanest fuel ever gets into the tank, and check the fuel filter element periodically – either cleaning it out or replacing it if necessary. At the same time, drain off the carburettor float chamber and look for any dirt.

Keep the circulating water inlet (and all other parts of the engine) clean and free of salt deposits. A wash down with fresh water and a coat of wax polish on painted surfaces will help protect the outer surfaces from corrosion.

While going round the engine take a careful look for any loose fastenings, worn insulation on electric leads, or leaks from hoses or their connections.

A SUBMERGED ENGINE

Should an engine be immersed, quick action is called for to minimise damage.

Assuming that it wasn't running when it submerged, begin by removing the cover and thoroughly washing the whole engine with fresh water. Disconnect the plug leads and remove the spark plugs. Disconnect and drain the fuel line and tank, drain the carburettor, and flush the whole fuel system with petrol before refilling the tank with the fuel/oil mixture recommended for breaking-in.

Lay the engine with the plug holes downwards, and turn the flywheel until no more water emerges. Squirt some outboard oil into the plug holes and spin the flywheel a few more times.

Thoroughly dry off all electrical equipment and connections – including the inside of the distributor cap, if the engine has one – and spray with WD40.

If possible, start the engine and run it for at least half an hour. If it won't start, it may help to remove the spark plugs, heat them up over a gas ring, and quickly put them back while still hot.

If the engine still won't start, take the plugs out again, and completely fill the engine with oil (any clean oil will do).

Alternatively, immerse the whole unit in clean fresh water to avoid direct exposure to the atmosphere.

The same procedure applies if the engine was running when it went overboard, except that if the engine is stiff to turn, you should not try to start it. It is possible that the connecting rods may have been bent by water in the cylinders stopping the pistons rising.

Similarly, be very wary of starting the engine if there are traces of sand or mud inside the cover, as grit in the crankcase will destroy the bearings almost instantaneously.

In any case the engine should be taken to a service centre as soon as possible.

10. MAINTENANCE

Paperwork – Tools – Spares – Day-to-day routines – Outboard engines – Routine maintenance

PAPERWORK

Every new engine comes with an owner's handbook, which should be carefully preserved. Although the standard of information and presentation varies somewhat from manufacturer to manufacturer, most of these publications are excellent – with clear and comprehensive descriptions of the various components and how to look after them. Most begin with a general description of the engine, with illustrations to identify the principal features. Then will probably follow technical data with such facts as bore, stroke, compression ratio, firing order, rated output and rpm, idling rpm, weight, engine rotation, specification and capacity of lubricating oil, fuel specification, valve clearances etc.

There will certainly be a section on operating procedures with descriptions of the controls and instruments, and covering how to start the engine, what to check while it is running, and how to stop it. Engine maintenance should cover all the procedures to be followed at set intervals, and a good handbook will have illustrations to show just what is involved with those items which an owner is expected to do on a routine basis. There may be a list of recommended spares and tools to be carried on board, and possibly a table showing the torque settings for the more important fasteners.

A section should be included on fault finding, and there ought to be a description of the procedure for laying up the engine for the winter and for returning it to service. There will almost certainly be a wiring diagram of the engine's electrical system. Some handbooks include a parts identification section, with illustrated part numbers of virtually every component – from the cylinder block to the smallest lock washer. Quite apart from the possible usefulness in ordering spares, the illustrations alone are very helpful in understanding how bits of the engine are put together.

From the above it is evident that a good engine handbook can be very informative – but only of course if it is read carefully and with understanding. Before even thinking of starting the engine, sit down quietly and read the handbook from cover to cover, and then read it again. If anybody else is to operate the engine make sure that they read it too. Try to obtain a second copy, one of course always remaining on board but the other at home so that if and when some problem arises you have the appropriate reference to hand.

With the documentation for a new engine comes a warranty card, on which various details such as the engine model and serial number, gearbox serial number, date of purchase, dealer, and the owner's name and address must be completed and returned immediately. Warranty claims will be dealt with more easily if the form has been returned and registered, so do this before starting the engine. Read the warranty carefully so that you know what is and what is not covered.

This is also the time to start some form of engine notebook for your own personal use. This should be kept ashore, and should contain any basic data that may be needed from time to time. For example, if writing a letter about the engine it may be inconvenient to have to go on board in order to determine the serial number of the gearbox. So examples of the sort of information that might be recorded are as follows:

Engine make/model/year/serial number.
Maximum horsepower/rpm; maximum continuous horsepower/rpm.
Fuel tank capacity.
Engine lubricating oil type and sump capacity.
Oil filter type/number.
Fuel filter type/number.
Gearbox make/model/year/serial number. Reduction ratio.
Gearbox oil type and capacity.
Any limitations on shaft trailing.
Shaft dimensions and material.
Propeller diameter/pitch/hand.
Batteries make/year/capacity.
Alternator make/model.
Starter make/model.
(Where fitted, similar details should be entered for an auxiliary generator set.)

If you can obtain one from the engine manufacturer or his dealer it will be helpful to hold a copy of the workshop manual for your engine. This will give a great deal of supplementary information that is not contained in the owner's handbook. For a start, it will provide a more comprehensive and detailed description of the engine and of its ancillary equipment, and it will give the procedures for stripping down the various parts of the engine, how to check and if necessary replace components, and how to rebuild the engine to its original standards.

However, the amateur boat owner-cum-mechanic should remember that such manuals are written primarily for qualified service technicians who are familiar not only with the product but with basic workshop practices. They have the right tools and test equipment to carry out the work involved, and they do not need instruction about blanking off openings as they dismantle the engine, about renewing gaskets or fastenings, about cleaning off faces on joints before assembly – or about a hundred and one other matters that come naturally to the trained mechanic. Remember too that your ambitious but unskilled work on the engine may invalidate the warranty. Nevertheless a workshop manual will certainly teach you more about the engine and help to pinpoint impending trouble. It

TIGHTENING TORQUES FOR A SABRE ENGINE

Fastening	Torque	
	lb/ft	Nm
Alternator adjusting bolt	18 to 20	24.4 to 27.1
Rocker shaft pedestal bolts	17 to 22	23 to 30
Fuel filter element retaining bolt	5 to 7	6.8 to 8.1
Injector retaining bolts	14 to 16	19 to 21.7
Injector pipe gland nut	12 to 15	17 to 20
Injector oil seal nut	16 to 20	22 to 27
Injector pipe union nut (pump end)	12 to 15	17 to 20
Injector leak-off pipe banjo bolt	12 to 14	17 to 19
Fuel filter bleed screws	5 to 7	7 to 10
Injection pump bleed screws	3 to 5	4 to 7
Manifold retaining bolts/nuts	17 to 22	23 to 29.8
Injection pump retaining bolts	25 to 27	33.9 to 36.6
Injection pump drive gear bolts	15 to 18	20 to 25
Water pump pulley bolts	16 to 18	22 to 25
Rocker cover screws	3 to 4	4 to 6

will also give a better understanding of the complexity of some of the work involved, and why the charges made for servicing and repair of engines is necessarily high, bearing in mind the range of tools, test equipment and spares which dealers have to carry.

The importance of using genuine spare parts needs to be emphasised, even with respect to what seem to be minor items such as nuts and bolts. A replacement bolt may look the same but is it exactly the right size, and is it the same material with equivalent strength? Two bolts can look deceptively similar and even have the same number of threads per inch (TPI), but the form of the thread may be different. Special locking bolts and nuts are often used for certain applications, so when stripping down components keep a careful check of which fastenings belong where and make sure they are replaced whence they came.

The more important fastenings in an engine must be tightened to the right torque – not too loose but at the same time not too tight so that threads are stretched and damaged, thus weakening the fastening. This requires the use of a suitable torque wrench, and it is necessary that the threads concerned are clean and lightly oiled (although sometimes a dry torque setting may be specified). Examples of torque settings for a Sabre diesel engine are shown in the table. Note for example the relatively low figures for rocker cover screws, bleed screws and the filter element retaining bolt.

Where two or more fastenings are used to secure the same part, never tighten individual nuts completely one at a time. First tighten them all to one-third of the final torque setting, then repeat at two-thirds of the setting, and then finally tighten to the full value. In many cases the order of tightening is important (in diagonal rather than radial sequence), a supreme example being in the case of tightening down a cylinder head where the precise order will be specified in the engine handbook.

TOOLS

It is impossible to work on or look after any engine

without a proper set of tools. Most manufacturers produce a recommended list of items required, and some will provide a more or less complete tool kit. Never buy cheap tools. The box contains a list of tools suggested by the makers for working on Sabre engines. The notation AF against the spanner sizes means 'across flats' – that is across two opposite flats of the hexagonal head. For engines built to metric standards these dimensions are shown in millimetres.

Spanner – open ended $7/16$in × $1/2$in AF
Spanner – open ended $1/2$in × $9/16$in AF
Spanner – open ended $5/8$in × $11/16$in AF
Spanner – open ended $3/4$in × $7/8$in AF
Spanner – open ended $15/16$in × 1in AF
Spanner – open ended $15/16$in × $1 1/2$in AF
Spanner – ring $1/4$in × $5/16$in AF
Spanner – ring $3/8$in × $7/16$in AF
Spanner – ring $1/2$in × $9/16$in AF
Spanner – ring $5/8$in × $11/16$in AF
Spanner, combination $15/16$in AF
Spanner, combination 13mm AF
Hacksaw, junior
Hexagon key set, $1/16$in – $3/8$in, 10 piece
Hexagon key set, 1.5–10mm, 10 piece
Screwdriver – cross slot
Socket set, $1/4$in to $3/4$in AF and 9 to 19mm, 24 piece
Spanner, $9/16$in × $5/8$in AF, open ring
Hammer – ball pein, 1 lb
Pliers – combination 8in
Spanner – adjustable 8in
Pliers – water pump 240mm
Screwdriver 8in
Screwdriver 5in
Feeler gauges, 4in × 10 blade
Tool bag

The list shown is intended only to cover routine maintenance as might normally be done by the owner, and for further work of an overhaul nature additional items are needed, starting with a torque wrench. Other items worth including are a small chain wrench or similar tool for gripping oil filter elements, a scraper for cleaning up joint faces and gaskets, vice or 'Mole' grips, a midget screwdriver for electrical work, needle-nose pliers, a Phillips screwdriver, round and flat files, and a set of Allen keys. Possibly some of these may not be needed for the actual engine, but the engine tool kit usually forms the boat's tool kit as well and all these items will come in useful on some occasion. Other things that are needed but which are perhaps not strictly tools include an oil can, a grease gun, a hydrometer and distilled water for the battery, light (3-in-1) oil, an aerosol of WD40, a selection of fastenings (nuts, bolts and washers) of different sizes, insulating tape, a test meter or lamp, jump leads, cable connectors, water pump grease and general purpose grease, sterntube packing, gasket material and plastic tubing in various sizes with suitable hose clips for emergency repairs.

Should you ever contemplate a top overhaul of the engine you will need a valve spring compressor, in order to remove the valves. If you have a problem with dirty injectors in a diesel engine, the best and simplest solution is to fit a spare set which should be carried on board. However, for a boat that makes extended cruises it is worth carrying a cleaning kit which has a brush with brass bristles for removing carbon, and brass prickers for clearing nozzle holes. Used carefully it should get you home if no spare injectors are available.

SPARES

The range of on-board spares that should be carried depends upon the intended use of the boat. More items are obviously needed for a boat which makes extended cruises than for one which only makes brief sorties by day from her home port. Engine manufacturers can usually recommend kits accordingly. As a minimum for coastal waters cruising the following are suggested:

Selection of gaskets; drive belt(s); oil filter element; fuel filter element; service kit for raw-water pump (including impeller); thermostat; selection of hoses and hose clips; lift pump repair kit; solenoid; air cleaner element; sacrificial anode(s) as fitted; fuses (as fitted).

In addition for diesel engines: a set of injectors and a set of high-pressure fuel pipes.

In addition for petrol engines: sparking plugs; contact breaker set; coil.

For outboard engines it is advisable to carry a spare propeller, and for small engines (where appropriate) a shear pin or spring drive.

When spares are required they may be needed in a hurry, so it is useful to have a list of what is on board and where each item is stowed. Some items such as hoses look very much alike, and should therefore be tallied for easy identification. A record must be kept of spares that are consumed so that they are re-ordered and properly stowed away. Resist the temptation to hoard old and useless items.

Apart from the mechanical spares above it is necessary to carry a full range of lubricants in sealed containers. Sufficient engine oil should be held for a complete oil change.

DAY-TO-DAY ROUTINES

Quite apart from the way that maintenance is scheduled in the engine handbook, there is another approach to the problem – who is to do it? Certain day-to-day routines fall inescapably to the lot of the boat owner – fairly simple and basic procedures but no less important for all that. If they are followed carefully many of the problems that can beset both petrol and diesel inboard engines can be forestalled.

Daily (or before getting underway)
Check fuel tank contents (preferably by dipstick and compare with fuel gauge reading) and record amount. In a small boat a reserve can of fuel is a sensible precaution, but if this is petrol it must be stowed in a metal container somewhere on deck – never down below. Compare fuel state with intended programme for the day. If in doubt, refuel. Note quantity taken.

Examine the bowl of the fuel filter and/or sedimenter for any contamination, which must be removed. With a diesel engine this may mean subsequent venting of the fuel system, but this should not deter you from the need to allow only the

Fig 1. Fuel filter servicing. Modern cartridge-type fuel filters are similar to cartridge oil filters, and can be removed in the same way – ideally using a chain or strap wrench. Have a bowl underneath to collect spillages. Lightly lubricate the rubber seal of the new cartridge, and screw it on hand-tight.

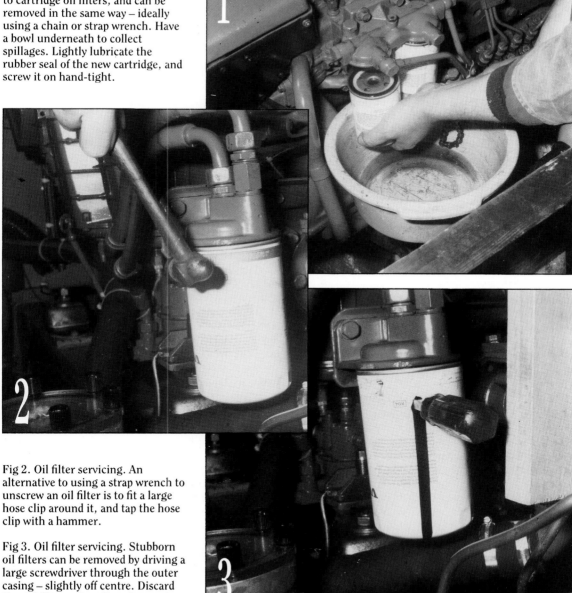

Fig 2. Oil filter servicing. An alternative to using a strap wrench to unscrew an oil filter is to fit a large hose clip around it, and tap the hose clip with a hammer.

Fig 3. Oil filter servicing. Stubborn oil filters can be removed by driving a large screwdriver through the outer casing – slightly off centre. Discard the old filter and sealing ring, and replace, tightening by hand only.

cleanest fuel to get into the system. Neglect of this basic point will only store up more serious and expensive problems.

Check lubricating oil level in engine sump. Top up if required, noting the quantity of oil added in the engine log book. Check the reserve stock of oil on board (in a cruising boat this should be enough for at least one complete filling). Oil consumption varies with the engine and how it is used, but for a diesel engine it is likely to be about one per cent of the fuel used, and a little higher while running in. It is useful to know how much oil is needed to raise the level from the 'low' to the 'full' marks on the dipstick. Do not overfill.

Check gearbox oil level. Note that with some gearboxes the level should be checked as soon as the engine has been stopped. A gearbox should seldom need replenishing, and if it does the cause should be investigated – probably a leaking oil seal at the aft end. This in turn may point to a problem with shaft alignment. Minor leaks are easier to detect if the exterior of the engine is kept spotlessly clean at all times.

Check the circulating water inlet strainer by visual examination. See that the seacock is open.

Where the engine has indirect (fresh-water) cooling, check the level in the header tank and top up if necessary with fresh water, as for a car radiator. Here again it is sensible to keep a record of the quantity added, since regular filling points to a leak somewhere – possibly into the engine which is a more serious matter than a minor leak outwards.

Check the bilge of the engine compartment for oil and/or water, and pump or bail out as necessary. Stop pumping before oil is discharged overboard. Any oily residue remaining must be removed by hand into a closed container and taken ashore for disposal. This job is a good deterrent for allowing oil leaks to develop or remain unattended. With a petrol engine check for any smell of petrol fumes in or around the engine compartment, but in any case run the exhaust fan that should be fitted for at least five minutes before starting the engine.

If so fitted (as for example in many auxiliary powered sailing cruisers) check that any valve on the exhaust line is open.

Check the battery state and close the main battery switches.

If the engine is not fitted with an hour meter record the time of starting (and stopping) so that an accurate record is kept of running hours. It is wise to check the operation of the hour meter from time to time.

Where fitted, operate sterntube greaser.

With a turbocharged engine which has not been used for some time, it may be necessary to prime the oil feed to the turbocharger by cranking the engine over with the stop control operating until pressure shows on the oil pressure gauge.

Before starting, check that the engine control is in neutral, single up mooring lines and check that there are no ropes or other obstructions near the propeller.

After starting

Check all instruments are reading normally (e.g. oil pressure gauge, ammeter, engine idling rpm).

Visually check cooling-water discharge overboard. Check ahead/neutral/astern operation of controls.

Do not leave the engine idling at the mooring or alongside. As soon as possible get underway and put the engine on load at moderate rpm to allow it to warm up. Only then should full power be used.

While under way

Keep a regular watch on all instruments. It is wise to keep a written record of key pressures and temperatures perhaps every 30 minutes. This is the only way to be sure of detecting any change from normal readings. A ruled book is needed with headings such as time, rpm, engine oil pressure, gearbox oil pressure, coolant temperature, charging amps, boost pressure and fuel contents.

Where fitted, operate sterntube greaser at required intervals.

Keep a close eye on fuel consumption.

Apart from watching the instruments a good skipper should be able to detect any change in the beat, sound or smell coming from the engine. These senses sometimes give the first sign of trouble developing.

Fig 4. To adjust valve clearances, turn the engine in the normal direction of rotation until the valve concerned is fully closed and the rocker or tappet is 'off the cam'. Slacken the lock nut (1), and hold it with a spanner. Insert the appropriate feeler gauge (2) between the valve stem and the rocker, and adjust the clearance with the screw (3). Hold the adjusting screw and tighten the lock nut before moving on to the next valve.

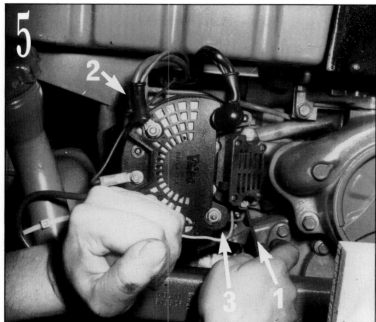

Fig 5. Adjusting the tension of the drive belt (1). The deflection should not exceed $\frac{1}{4}$in (6mm). Slacken the alternator pivot bolt (2), and adjusting bolt (3); use a piece of wood to lever the alternator outwards to correct the tension, and tighten the bolts.

On return to or arrival in harbour

Before stopping a turbocharged engine let it idle for a couple of minutes to allow the turbocharger to slow down.

With a diesel engine, pull the spring loaded stop control until the engine ceases to rotate, and then make sure it returns to the 'run' position.

Record engine hours and fuel remaining. If possible refuel before leaving the boat for any length of time.

Close the seawater inlet seacock.

Check bilge levels.

Break main battery switches. With a petrol engine (only) shut fuel cock.

Make a note of any defects to be rectified, however small.

OUTBOARD ENGINES

The sorts of day-to-day jobs needed for an outboard are necessarily somewhat different, even though many of the basic principles above still apply. When an outboard is stopped, make a habit of tilting the engine so that the propeller is above water. This minimises the chance of water leaking into the lower unit. Check the oil level in the lower unit regularly, both for quantity and quality, and drain it off and refill it at least every season. Pivot points and linkages must be lubricated monthly with a good marine grease. Remember that the engine must never be started unless the lower unit is immersed in water, or damage will be caused to the water pump impeller.

ROUTINE MAINTENANCE

In addition to day-to-day jobs there are certain important routines which have to be carried out at intervals – either on a basis of engine running hours or time in months, whichever comes first. Here we are not concerned with the details of the work, which will be given in the engine handbook, but rather with some form of documentation in order to record what has been done and when, and to plan what will be due in the near future. This should avoid discovering that an oil change is due just before setting off on a summer cruise.

When planning maintenance it is better to arrange for several items to be taken in hand on one day. In the long run this saves a bit of time in gaining access to the engine, assembling tools and lubricants, cleaning up afterwards, and running the engine to check the work. Although this may mean sacrificing a day's use of the boat at least the work can be done at a more leisurely pace (and probably more thoroughly) than when trying to catch the afternoon tide. Jobs do not always go according to plan and may take longer than expected.

In a twin-screw boat it is necessary to remember that the maintenance load is doubled so far as the engines are concerned. If the boat is at anchor, or on a mooring in bad weather, it is wise to dismantle only one engine at a time in case it is necessary to get under way. This reminds one of the need to practise handling a twin-screw boat on one shaft, which requires a different technique for close-quarter manoeuvring.

Whenever any work is done on an engine first make sure that it is clean externally, so that no dirt can get inside. Fuel pipes etc must be sealed when disconnected (plastic caps are useful for this). Be methodical, so that each component is replaced exactly where it came from. Set aside a clean area so that all the pieces can be laid out in their correct relative positions. Before the components are reassembled make sure that they are thoroughly clean. Check all threads for any sign of damage, and lightly oil them. See that all joint faces are cleaned off and, if necessary, renew any gasket or joint ring. Make sure that all blanks that may have been fitted temporarily are removed, and that no small bits of rag are left inside the engine. On completion always run the engine to make certain that there are no leaks and that everything is functioning normally.

11. TRIALS, TUNING AND WINTER CARE

Commissioning trials – Revolutions, speed and fuel consumption – Engine tuning – Laying up inboard engines – Recommissioning – Outdrives and outboards

COMMISSIONING TRIALS

Full commissioning trials of an engine require sophisticated instrumentation usually only available on a manufacturer's test bed. So once an engine has been installed in a boat it is too late to carry out comprehensive trials. The builder might check that the machinery is in working order, but such trials can never tell you how well it is working, nor whether it is coming up to spec.

So it is worth doing your own trials on a new engine. Start with a visual inspection, checking all wiring and pipe connections and removing any packing materials and tape. Make sure that the controls are operating properly, that there is enough oil and coolant, and that the raw-water seacock is open.

Then start the engine, and while it is running at a fast tickover – about 800rpm for a big diesel, or up to about 1500rpm for a small petrol engine – check that cooling water is flowing, and that the charge warning light has gone out. The oil pressure gauge should initially show about 45lb/in^2 (3.16kg/cm^2) or more, but may fall slightly at idling speed as the oil warms up.

During initial trials, access to the engine should be left open, so that you can see what is going on.

Until the coolant reaches about 140°F (60°C) only moderate rpm should be used. Then, if all is satisfactory, run for very short periods at full power. Manufacturers' instructions will vary, but in general it is inadvisable to run at full power for more than about 5 minutes at a time until 10 hours' running have been achieved.

Record the following data: idling rpm in neutral (engine hot); maximum governed rpm in neutral; and engine rpm, boost pressure, coolant temperature, oil pressure, and boat speed at maximum power under way. Because the boat speed will partly depend on the all-up weight, you should also note the fuel and water tank gauge readings and the number of people on board. Finally, examine the installation for fuel, oil or water leaks.

REVOLUTIONS, SPEED AND FUEL CONSUMPTION

Most manufacturers assign two or more power ratings to each engine, adjusting or adapting the fuel injection equipment to give the required engine speed and torque to suit each of several types of use.

An engine intended to produce, for example, 190hp (142kW) at 2200rpm for a fishing boat or ferry in continuous use, might well be adapted to develop 230hp (172kW) at 2500rpm for the lighter 'duty cycle' of a pilot cutter or police launch. While for a motor cruiser or rescue boat, used for only a few hours a year and only intermittently at full power, its rating might be further increased to 300hp (224kW) at 2800rpm.

Engine power curves, published by the manufacturer, are a useful basis on which to start documenting the performance of your own particular engine. But remember that these curves of power output, torque and specific fuel consumption are obtained with the engine on test at full load and under standard conditions of temperature and atmospheric pressure. If, for example, the temperature in the engine space is unduly high because of

ESTIMATING FUEL CONSUMPTION

The rate at which an engine burns fuel depends on the sophistication of its design and manufacture. In general, modern engines are much more fuel efficient than those produced just ten years ago. There are rules of thumb, however, which can be used to estimate full-speed consumption.

A diesel engine married to the right propeller and running flat out, will burn about 0.05 gallons of fuel per hour per horsepower. Under the same conditions, a petrol engine uses about 0.10 gallons per hour per horsepower.

Having estimated your fuel consumption at full revs, the corresponding figures for lower speeds can be worked out from the graph.

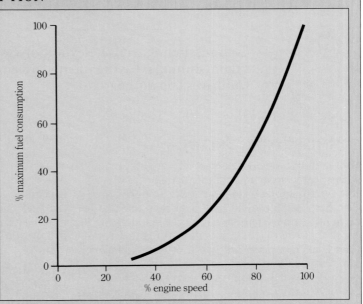

inadequate ventilation, then engine performance will suffer.

If the boat's propulsive system has been correctly designed and installed she will attain her intended speed with the engine developing the maximum rated speed. In a planing boat this may involve experimenting with several propellers to get optimum performance under operating conditions when the hull resistance is increased by extra displacement or fouling of the bottom.

Just as important – or in some applications even more important – is that the boat should have a realistic economical cruising speed. This depends not only on the engine but on the design of the hull, and it too will need to be determined by experiment.

And for the owner who uses a boat for serious cruising it is essential to establish and understand the relationships between boat speed, engine rpm, fuel consumption and range.

The best way to start performance trials is by plotting a graph of boat speed against engine rpm. Most boats have electronic logs to measure speed and distance run, but these are not always accurate and sometimes not very reliable. More accurate results can be obtained by using a stopwatch to measure the time taken to cover a measured distance.

Measured distances, marked by two pairs of transit beacons, are set up at many places round our coasts, but even if there isn't one in your area, it is not too difficult to make alternative arrangements by taking the distance between two fixed points such as piers or beacons from the chart. Or a radar range can be taken on some fixed object.

In any case it is essential to allow for any tidal set by making at least one run in each direction, recording the time taken, the engine rpm, the log speed and distance readings, and a general note of the wind and sea state.

Assuming that a measured distance is used, first check its actual length on the chart: some are not an exact nautical mile. Having completed both runs at a fixed throttle setting, work out the speed achieved on each run, and from these calculate the average speed. If four runs have been completed at a particular throttle setting, an even more reliable result can be obtained by taking the 'mean of means': multiply the successive speeds by 1, 2, 2 and 1 and then divide the total obtained by six.

Runs at very low speeds are not particularly fruitful and can take a long time, so it is best to concentrate on runs at half-speed and above. In a 20-knot boat, for example, aim to select engine revs that will give about 12, 14, 16, 18 and 20 knots.

Fuel consumption figures are more difficult to get, and may take some time, but it is well worth the effort. When setting off on any passage that can be made at a constant speed (the longer the better), top up the fuel to the brim. On arrival, check how much fuel is needed to fill up, and hence how much has been consumed on passage. It is also necessary to record the time on passage, wind and sea state, boat loading, condition of bottom – and of course the engine rpm used. It is particularly important to try to get figures about the likely economical cruising speed, in order to determine what this actually is.

All this information needs to be tabulated in some way – Figs 1, 2, 3 and 4 show one method – and kept near the helm for easy reference. Twin-engined boats need two such charts – one showing performance with both engines, the other with one engine only.

A reliable fuel gauge is important, and this can be checked periodically when the boat is refuelled.

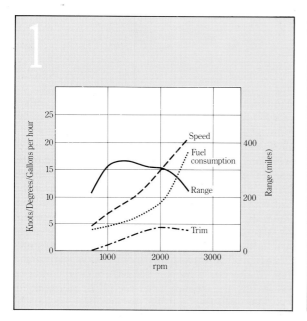

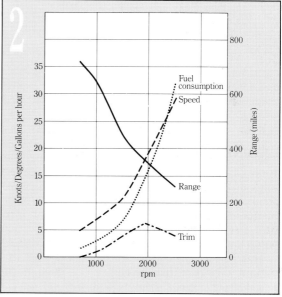

Fig 1. Curves of speed, consumption, range and trim angle plotted against engine rpm for a deep-vee motor cruiser, with twin 188hp (140kW) diesels and a fuel capacity of 240 gallons (1091l) – assuming 20% fuel left in reserve.

Fig 2. Corresponding curves for a somewhat larger deep-vee motor cruiser, powered by two 357hp (266kW) diesels, and with a fuel capacity of 360 gallons (1637l) – again with 20% fuel remaining.

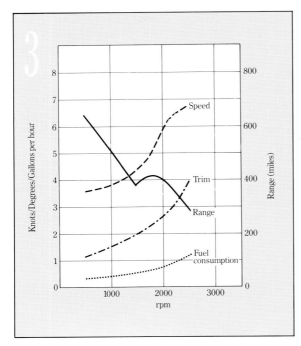

Fig 3. Another marked change, in the curves for a traditional motorsailer of 34ft l.o.a., with a 47hp (35kW) engine and 66 gallons (300l) of fuel (20% reserve).

Fig 4. And for a more modern 35ft motorsailer with a 43hp (32kW) engine and 88 gallons (400l) of fuel (20% reserve).

ENGINE TUNING

Tuning is simply the process of getting all the settings of the engine into the right adjustment for good and economical performance. It covers such matters as valve timing, ignition timing and mixture strength on a petrol engine, and injection pump timing and the setting of injectors in a diesel.

But before sorting out these details it is important to be sure that the engine is in good mechanical order. Here a compression test can give a general indication. This is done with a special pressure gauge with an adaptor to fit in place of an injector or a spark plug as the case may be. Each cylinder is tested in turn, either while the engine is running, or while it is being turned over with the starter.

Poor compression on all cylinders is likely to be caused either by worn piston rings or cylinder bore, or by leaking valves. Valve problems may be due to a build-up of carbon or wear on the seat, the valve sticking in the guide, a defective valve spring, or wrong valve clearance. Whether valves or rings are to blame may be found by pouring a very small quantity of oil into the cylinder and repeating the test. If there is a substantial improvement (due to oil sealing the clearance between the rings and the cylinder wall) the fault lies there: otherwise look to the valves.

Very poor compression on one cylinder alone indicates a blown cylinder head gasket, or a cracked head or block, while poor compression on two adjacent cylinders points towards a blown gasket between two affected cylinders.

The best tuning can be achieved, and much time saved, by using portable electronic test equipment. Particularly for a petrol engine, useful readings can be taken with the engine actually running. The battery level and general state of the electrical system, alternator performance, low tension voltage at the coil, dwell angle (the crankshaft angle over which the breaker points are closed), the points condition, the voltage at each plug in turn, ignition timing and automatic advance, and the accuracy of the engine tachometer, can all be checked. If a problem is detected the tester can be used to locate the fault by making tests of individual components.

As described in chapter 3, carburettors are delicate items, and their correct adjustment is essential for good engine performance. With continued use clearances alter and may need to be restored. The procedure should be given in the engine handbook or workshop manual, and must be followed strictly. Particularly where two or more carburettors are fitted to an engine it is best to leave this work to an expert.

Diesel engine test equipment may examine the performance of the fuel pump and of individual injectors under operating conditions. But although fuel injection pump timing, and idling speed, can be adjusted on the engine, other work on the fuel system such as calibration of the injection pump or setting the operating pressures of individual injectors can only be done in a workshop.

The equipment required is too expensive to be worth buying for private use, but a growing number of companies are offering a mobile testing facility: the process is so quick and effective that it may well work out cheaper than attempting DIY diagnosis, which almost inevitably involves an element of trial and error.

LAYING UP

Many owners never use their boat in the winter — leaving the engine vulnerable to corrosion and frost damage.

Even if you have to employ a boatyard to winterise the engine, it is worth doing as it will save money in the long run. However, the job is quite

simple and well within the capacity of the average owner.

Because most pleasure craft run for very few hours during a season, laying up can often be combined with much of the routine servicing, while the winter months provide the opportunity to undertake a whole range of more major tasks such as cleaning and painting, cleaning fuel tanks, or improving the installation by adding sound-proofing or suppressing radio interference.

The engine handbook should give full details of what has to be done for your particular engine, but an idea of what is involved is given below.

Some of the operations are inter-related, so it is necessary to plan the right sequence of events quite carefully, and to ensure that the right tools, lubricants, spares and equipment are all to hand when needed. Good preparation will save a lot of time and effort!

Thinking well ahead pays particular dividends in respect of fuel state. Diesel tanks are best left full during the winter to minimise condensation inside, so refuel at the last possible moment before lifting or hauling out, and add a biocide to inhibit the possible growth of 'diesel bugs' if you are in an area where they are known to be a problem.

Petrol tanks, on the other hand, should be left empty, so it is advisable to run down the amount on board to the bare minimum before laying up.

LAYING UP INBOARD ENGINES

Check engine condition by running at full power and reading instruments. If possible test compression, and use electronic test equipment to check engine tune.

Clean and degrease exterior. Make good damaged paint.

Run engine until warm. Change engine oil and oil filter. Clean breather pipe. (Note: for an extended lay-up use an inhibiting oil, which must be replaced before the engine is put back into service.)

Diesels

Check tank contents are clean and free from water. Clean separator and change fuel filter. Disconnect lift pump suction pipe and lead it into a container filled with a 2:1 mixture of clean diesel fuel and an inhibiting oil. (Note: there are different types of inhibiting oils and rust preventives. Be sure to get one, such as Esso Rust Ban 335, suitable for diesel fuel systems.) Bleed the fuel system ready for starting. Remove and service air cleaner.

Cooling systems

With the boat ashore or alongside, flush through the raw-water system by leading the pump suction to a container that holds about four gallons, such as a small dustbin, kept topped up with a hose. (Never connect a hose direct to the cooling system.) In direct cooling systems, remove the thermostat. Run the engine at a low speed to flush the cooling system, circulate clean lubricating oil, and (in a diesel engine) feed the fuel/inhibiting oil mixture through the fuel injection system. After about ten minutes (before running out of fuel) turn off the hose and allow the level in the container to drop to about two gallons. Pour in one gallon (five litres) of a soluble oil (e.g. Shell Dromus B or Esso Kutwell 42) and stir well. Then, once the inhibiting mixture has been sucked into the system, stop the engine.

Remove the raw-water pump impeller. Unless it is in excellent condition, renew it in the spring. Drain down the raw-water system. Drain cocks may need clearing, and it may be necessary to break hose connections. Check any corrosion pieces

Fig 5. Some of the items associated with laying up a six-cylinder diesel engine, turbocharged with intercooler: (1) lubricating oil filter; (2) sump drain pump; (3) breather pipe; (4) fuel filter; (5) raw-water circulating pump; (6) heat exchanger; (7) injector; (8) sump dipstick; (9) gearbox filler/dipstick; (10) coolant filler/pressure cap; (11) oil filler cap; (12) water outlet from exhaust manifold; (13) air filter (turbocharger inlet); (14) turbocharger exhaust outlet; (15) intercooler; (16) gearbox oil cooler; (17) propeller shaft coupling; (18) engine oil cooler.

fitted. (Note: an alternative procedure is to flush the raw-water system with a mixture of anti-freeze instead of soluble oil.)

With fresh-water cooling, drain the coolant from heat exchanger and block. Remove the thermostat and flush with fresh water. Undertake whatever maintenance is needed on heat exchangers, which need cleaning every year in dirty or muddy waters. Refill system with recommended mixture of anti-freeze.

Petrol engines

Clean the filters and drain the lift pump and carburettor. Remove the spark plugs and squirt a little inhibiting oil into each cylinder. Turn the engine a couple of revolutions and replace the plugs.

Miscellaneous

Remove the drive belt and examine for wear. Clean off pulleys and spray with WD40 to prevent rust, which will wear out the belt. Blank off the air inlet and exhaust connections on the engine.

Clean off terminals of battery, starter and alternator and smear with petroleum jelly. Store the battery in a cool, dry place free from frost. Top up with distilled water and charge monthly.

Clean and grease all exposed metal parts, control linkages etc. Spray electrical components with WD40.

Clean off and inhibit all accessible parts of propeller shafting. For an extended lay-up remove the sterngland packing. Check for propeller damage, and if it is removed grease the exposed shafting. Check clearance of shaft in sterntube and shaft bracket.

RECOMMISSIONING

Replace or renew drive belts and check tension.

Replace or renew raw-water pump impeller and open seacock.

Remove all blanks, tape etc fitted for the winter. Clean air filter.

Check engine oil level. If laid up with inhibiting oil in the sump, this must be replaced. Check gearbox oil level.

Check all drain cocks are closed and hose connections tight. Check coolant level.

For petrol engine, fit new spark plugs with correct gap, check and adjust contact breaker gap, clean distributor.

For diesel engine, fit serviced injectors.

Clean off excess petroleum jelly from electrical terminals. Fit charged battery (correct polarity).

If propeller shaft coupling has been broken, check alignment with the boat afloat. Fill sterntube greaser (where fitted).

Check fuel tank contents. Prime fuel system.

For diesel engine, particularly turbocharged, prime the oil system by cranking engine over.

Run engine similar to commissioning trials.

OUTDRIVES AND OUTBOARDS

Much of the procedure for inboards applies to outdrives and outboards, although there may be differences in the methods employed.

Outdrives and outboards should be stored with their legs down, and, in the case of outboards, supported on the normal mounting (not standing on the skeg).

Larger outboards may have a special attachment for flushing the cooling system, but for smaller units the simplest method is to mount the engine with the leg in a dustbin which is filled with a hose.

With both outdrives and outboards it is advisable to drain and refill the gearcase each winter.

Clean the leg and touch up any damaged paintwork, but do not paint the zinc anode(s).

The drive bellows of outdrive units should be checked carefully and renewed every four years unless otherwise specified. Splits or wear could sink the boat, or cause expensive damage to the gears.

With two-stroke petrol outboards the fuel system should be drained completely, to avoid a gummy deposit forming during the winter.

12. TROUBLESHOOTING

Starting a diesel engine – Starting a petrol engine – Trouble in service – Misfiring – Overloading and overheating – Sudden stopping – Long-term troubles – Gearboxes – Outboard engines

If an engine is reluctant to start or is not running smoothly, it's no good just hoping that it will be better next week: the chances are that it will get worse. It is much better to sort out problems as they arise – even if professional help is needed, it will probably save you money by avoiding more expensive repairs later on, and it could save you from an embarrassing breakdown at sea.

STARTING A DIESEL ENGINE

A diesel engine is relatively simple. If the air in the cylinder is compressed and thereby heated sufficiently, and if the fuel is then correctly injected, the engine should start and run.

The most likely cause of failure to start is a low cranking speed, possibly aggravated by cold weather. Low cranking speed leaves more time for both compression and heat to be lost. At the same time, cold air needs to be heated more to reach ignition temperature, while the metal of a cold engine absorbs more of the heat that has been generated by compression. The situation is further aggravated if the engine is not in good mechanical order – with leaking valves or piston rings for example.

So when an engine is reluctant to start in cold weather, anything that will heat or speed it up will help.

Most cold starting aids work by raising the temperature of the fuel, the air, or the engine, but if the cold-start device alone is not enough some other source of heat must be found. Even in a diesel's engine compartment, a naked flame is asking for trouble, but if the compartment has been well ventilated, a propane torch waved across the air inlet may do the trick. A small quantity of oily waste or rags could be burnt to achieve the same result, but if such drastic remedies are used make sure that there is nothing flammable nearby, and have an extinguisher handy. A safer alternative is a paraffin safety heater, left burning in the engine compartment overnight, or better still an electric lamp or small heater running on a shore power supply.

Ether starting aids operate by injecting a small quantity of ether into the inlet manifold. Ether's low flash point (ignition temperature) means that it will burn much more readily than diesel. Once the ether has ignited, of course, it sets fire to the diesel spray from the injectors.

Aerosol sprays are available for the same purpose, but it is all too easy to exceed the dose, causing severe pre-ignition and possibly damaging the engine.

Twin-engine installation are usually fitted with a parallelling switch, connecting the two banks of batteries so that both batteries can be used to start one engine, increasing its cranking speed.

Turning the engine over by hand can reduce oil drag, and warming a battery – ideally by putting it on charge in a warm place – can help maintain the cranking speed. The engine cranking speed can be increased if the air inlet is temporarily blanked off with a piece of plywood or stout cardboard – restricting the air supply and reducing the compression until the engine reaches starting speed.

And a naturally-aspirated engine can sometimes be coaxed into starting with a squirt of oil into the air inlet while turning the engine over: the oil will help seal the piston rings and help build up compression.

STARTING PETROL ENGINES

Although the lower compression ratio of a petrol engine is less demanding of its battery and starter than a diesel, it still will not start unless it is turned over at sufficient speed.

But assuming that the starter turns the engine satisfactorily the most likely causes of non-starting lie either in the ignition system or the fuel system.

As a first step, if the engine has been turned over on the starter for a while, it is probably flooded with petrol. Slowly open the throttle and choke, and leave the engine alone for a while to let the petrol vaporise before trying to start it again, this time with the throttle in its normal starting position and the choke open.

Should it still not start it is time to check the ignition system at one of the spark plugs. Disconnect the lead and – holding it with a clothes peg or insulated pliers – hold the terminal about ⅛in (3mm) from the cylinder head, and crank the engine once more. A good spark should jump across the gap. If it does, the ignition system is obviously working, but it is still advisable to remove the plugs to check their condition, and make certain that the plug leads are connected in the right sequence.

This simple check virtually eliminates ignition defects as the cause of the trouble: it is possible that the timing may be out, but this is unlikely unless the engine has just been overhauled.

Finding and rectifying faults on an electronic ignition system which fails this test requires special equipment and a trained operator. The owner can do no more than ensure that all the connections are clean and tight.

Coil ignition systems are more prone to faults, but very much easier to put right. It is important to be methodical.

If there is no spark at the plug lead, trace the system back, looking first at the HT circuit. Remove the HT lead from the centre of the distributor cap and hold it – with insulated pliers – close to a good earth point while the engine is cranked over. If there is a spark the fault lies in the distributor: in the rotor arm or the central carbon brush at the top. If there is no spark then the trouble is either in the coil or in the LT circuit.

Turn the engine over by hand so that the contact breaker points are closed. Switch on the ignition and flick the points open with a small piece of wood. If a small spark jumps the gap between the points, well and good, but if it is a hefty spark and the contact breaker points are burnt the condenser may be faulty.

Further tests on the LT circuit are best done with a test lamp or voltmeter fitted with a clip on one terminal and a probe on the other. Attach the clip to earth and place the probe at the terminal where the LT lead from the distributor joins the coil (at point D in Fig 1), and turn the engine over with the ignition on. If the light goes on and off the contact breaker is functioning, but if it stays on, the contact breaker points are not opening. If there is no light, either there is a break in the LT circuit or a short-circuit to earth in the condenser or contact breaker wiring.

Disconnect the wire from the terminal at A and put it to the end of the probe. If the lamp lights then the LT circuit is intact up to that point, and the fault is in the contact breaker. If it does not, the fault can be found by moving the test probe progressively round the circuit to B, C and D in the diagram. For example if the light shows with the probe at C but not at D, the primary (LT) winding of the coil is defective.

Only once ignition problems have been eliminated is it worth considering the fuel system.

Check the most obvious things first: is there fuel in the tank (the gauge may be wrong) and is the fuel cock open? Disconnect the fuel pipe at the carburettor, and see whether fuel is delivered when the fuel pump is operated. If no fuel appears there may be a blockage in the fuel line or primary filter.

An alternative possibility is a defective fuel pump. Fuel pumps are normally engine driven, so the most likely failure is the flexible diaphragm which actually does the pumping.

If fuel is being delivered, any fault must lie in

Fig 1. Checking the ignition system of
a petrol engine.

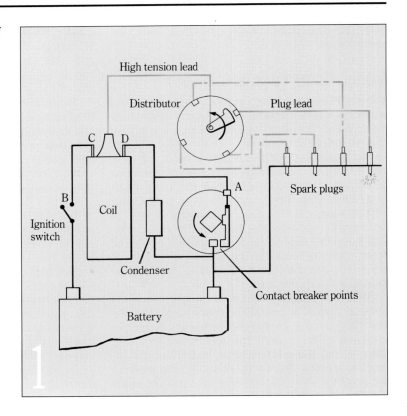

the carburettor itself. This is such a delicate component that adjustments are best left to a mechanic, but it is useful to check that its various linkages are working correctly, and to open up the float chamber to check the internal cleanliness and the operation of the float-controlled needle valve.

If yours is a variable-jet carburettor, check that the piston which controls the position of the needle valve is free to operate in its housing, and top up its oil damper.

TROUBLE IN SERVICE

Unless it runs out of fuel an engine seldom stops without some warning. A change of beat indicates misfiring; fluctuating speed points to partial fuel starvation – or perhaps a defective governor in the case of a diesel – while metallic sounds or squeaks herald some mechanical problem.

A good sense of smell also helps. It is not too difficult to differentiate between hot lubricating oil, escaping fuel, and the acrid smell of hot electrical equipment. Practical engineers rely on their sense of touch (how long they can hold their hand on a bearing for example) to check temperatures. Feel your way around your own engine as it warms up so that you know what to expect. Even taste can sometimes be helpful, perhaps to distinguish between salt or fresh water in the event of contamination.

MISFIRING

When an engine is misfiring the first step is to discover which cylinder is at fault. On a petrol engine, earth each plug terminal in turn with a screwdriver, or remove each plug cap in turn. On a diesel, slacken the high-pressure fuel pipe at each injector in turn. The plug or injector which has no effect on the beat of the engine is the culprit.

Misfiring can be due to a number of causes. Obviously it pays to investigate the more likely causes first. With a diesel these are a leaking injector pipe, a faulty (dirty) injector, or a sticking valve.

General rough running in a diesel, not related to any particular cylinder, may be due to air in the fuel or, more sinister, to water or dirt which require urgent action to prevent damage to injection equipment. Another possible cause may be poor compression.

Having identified one faulty cylinder in a petrol engine, it is unlikely that the cylinder in question is the only one not receiving fuel, so initially check the spark from the lead at the plug terminal. If that is satisfactory, check the plug – if it's okay, that eliminates the ignition system. If there is not a good spark, check the plug lead and the distributor. If this results in a healthy spark at the plug but that cylinder is still missing, it is time to check its compression for possible valve trouble. If possible, turn the engine over by hand to check the compression, and remove the rocker gear cover to see whether one valve is stuck: a little penetrating oil may free it, if only temporarily.

OVERLOADING AND OVERHEATING

Once an engine in reasonable mechanical order has been started, it should carry on running so long as it is fed with clean fuel and clean cooling water – and providing it is used sensibly and is not overloaded.

Overloading, indicated by the engine failing to reach its intended speed, or possibly even stopping altogether, can be caused by a fouled propeller, a very dirty bottom, the boat being physically overloaded, the wrong propeller, towing another boat, or single-engine operation of a twin-screw boat.

Overheating is a more serious matter, but provided it is detected early, before any damage is done to the engine, it is usually no more than an inconvenience which is easy to resolve – the commonest cause is a blocked raw-water strainer.

If a check of strainer, pumps, header tank and thermostat does not reveal the problem it is necessary to look elsewhere. Start with the oil level in the sump. Too small a quantity may still register a pressure but will tend to overheat, so that the working parts of the engine get too hot. This should be detectable from a drop in oil pressure as the oil gets thinner.

Other possible causes of overheating include a dirty air cleaner, a faulty injection pump or faulty injectors in the case of a diesel engine, incorrect valve timing, a restriction in the exhaust pipe, a leaking cylinder head gasket, or the need for a general overhaul. An engine which is raw-water cooled may have its cooling passages blocked with salt or silt.

SUDDEN STOPPING

When a diesel engine suddenly stops or splutters to a halt without any outward signs from the instruments, it is almost certain that the problem is shortage of fuel, or air or dirt in the system. Air or dirt may get into the system if the tank level is allowed to get too low in bad weather.

If a petrol engine stops suddenly, look to the ignition system first (although a total fuel failure can show the same symptoms). Gradual spluttering to a standstill, with a spitting carburettor, indicates fuel starvation.

LONG-TERM TROUBLES

With their low running hours, pleasure craft engines should not normally experience major failures. Some of the problems which might eventually arise are shown in the tables, together with probable causes.

Even if rectification is beyond the skill of the owner, it is still important to notice the symptoms, so as to be able to pass on relevant information to the service engineer who will have to diagnose the trouble.

Exhaust smoke, especially from a diesel, is a sign of an unhealthy engine. Black smoke, composed of particles of unburnt fuel, is usually caused

DIESEL ENGINES

Symptoms

Symptoms	Possible causes (see key below)
Engine runs intermittently (starts and stops)	1, 2, 3, 4, 5, 6, 7
Rough idling	1, 2, 3, 4, 7, 8, 9, 10, 11
Misfiring	2, 3, 7, 8, 10, 11, 13, 14, 15, 16, 17, 18, 19, 20, 31
Knocking	2, 7, 8, 9, 10, 11, 13, 15, 18, 19, 21, 22, 31
Engine not developing full power	2, 3, 4, 6, 7, 8, 10, 13, 14, 15, 16, 17, 18, 19, 20, 23, 24, 27, 29
Black exhaust smoke	6, 7, 8, 10, 14, 15, 16, 17, 19, 20, 23, 24, 25, 27, 31
White exhaust smoke	2, 10, 12, 15, 16, 17, 29, 31
Blue exhaust smoke	13, 23, 28, 30

Possible causes

1. Idling adjustment too low
2. Air in fuel system
3. Fuel filter choked
4. Fuel lift pump defective
5. Fuel tank nearly empty
6. Dirty air cleaner
7. Sticking valves or rocker arms
8. Dirty or faulty injectors
9. Broken valve spring(s)
10. Wrong injection pump timing
11. Injector pipe(s) loose or defective
12. Water in fuel
13. Defective or sticking piston rings/worn cylinder bores
14. Faulty fuel injection pump
15. Incorrect valve timing
16. Poor compression
17. Leaking cylinder head gasket
18. Engine overheating
19. Incorrect valve (tappet) clearances
20. Defective valves or seats
21. Low oil pressure
22. Defective bearings
23. Worn valve guides
24. Dirty or damaged turbocharger
25. Engine overloaded (e.g. wrong propeller or dirty bottom)
26. Defective boost control
27. Exhaust pipe restriction
28. Crankcase overfilled
29. Engine overcooled
30. Leaking turbocharger oil seal
31. Faulty cold start equipment

by overloading, defective injection equipment, or a blocked air filter. White smoke is due to the engine being overcooled (e.g. when starting up), or perhaps to water in the fuel. Blue smoke, whether from a diesel or a petrol engine, comes from burning lubricating oil which can get into the combustion chamber past worn piston rings or valve guides.

GEARBOXES

Gearboxes are complex assemblies, but are generally reliable. The most likely trouble stems from incorrect adjustment of the cable control, where the travel of the selector lever on the gearbox must exactly follow the movement of the lever at the helm.

They need correct lubrication and adjustment of the ahead/astern clutches or brake band to prevent slipping and consequent overheating. With some more simple gearboxes the adjustment of the brake band or clutches is not too difficult given the right tools, and should be described in the handbook.

In hydraulic gearboxes, lack of oil or dirty oil causes loss of pressure to operate the clutch, and loss of drive. Some can be locked in ahead gear mechanically, as an emergency measure.

PETROL ENGINES

Symptoms

Symptoms	Possible causes (see key below)
Engine stalls	When cold: 1, 2, 15, 26. When hot: 3, 4, 5, 6, 7, 8, 10, 15, 26
Rough idling	4, 5, 6, 8, 9, 10, 15, 16, 23, 25
Misfiring	6, 7, 8, 9, 10, 11, 15, 19, 26, 27
Knocking (pinking)	10, 21, 22, 23, 24
Engine not developing full power	6, 8, 9, 10, 11, 13, 15, 16, 17, 18, 19, 20, 25, 26, 27
Poor acceleration	5, 6, 8, 10, 11, 12, 13, 14, 15, 16, 17, 18, 19, 25, 26, 27
Engine 'runs on'	8, 10, 15, 22, 23, 24

Possible causes

1. Choke/throttle stop needs adjusting
2. Choke not operating
3. Idling speed set too low
4. Idling fuel mixture wrong
5. Choke operating incorrectly
6. Breaker points worn or dirty
7. Carburettor flooding
8. Air leak on inlet manifold
9. Sparking plugs need attention (dirty, wrong gap or cracked insulator)
10. Incorrect ignition timing
11. Fuel shortage at carburettor
12. Accelerator pump faulty
13. Dirty air cleaner
14. Seized piston (variable jet carburettor)
15. Valve (tappet) clearances need adjusting
16. Poor compression
17. Throttle control needs adjusting
18. Automatic advance not functioning
19. Ignition fault
20. Carburettor needs cleaning
21. Wrong grade of fuel
22. Engine overheating
23. Deposits in combustion chamber (needs top overhaul)
24. Wrong grade of sparking plug
25. Worn cylinder bores/rings/valve guides
26. Water or dirt in petrol
27. Valve(s) sticking, or broken valve spring(s)

OUTBOARD ENGINES

Although the great majority of outboards are two-stroke engines running on a petrol/oil mixture, the same safety precautions and basic principles apply to their starting, ignition, and fuel systems as to a petrol engine.

When working on an outboard bear in mind that the engine cover is not just to keep water away but is also a machinery guard. A spinning flywheel can be very dangerous. It is also possible for an engine to start accidentally when the flywheel or propeller is turned. So always make sure that the ignition is off, and remove the spark plug leads.

Larger outboards usually have an interlock to prevent the engine from being started unless the gear shift is in neutral: this, and the emergency ignition cut-off are the first things to check in the event of starting difficulties.

Next check the fuel supply from the remote tank (or on a small engine with an integral tank see that the fuel cock and the vent on the filler cap are both open). The fuel hose must be properly connected with no leaks and with no kinks in it, and the primer squeezed until a firm pressure is felt in the bulb. If there is still no fuel reaching the carburettor have a look at the filter.

If the engine still does not start, check the ignition by testing the spark at a plug, as for a four-stroke engine. If the spark is satisfactory examine the plugs, which are more susceptible to fouling in a two-stroke. A wet plug shows that the engine has been flooding. Open the throttle and the choke and let it stand for five minutes before trying again. If flooding persists look at the carburettor for the reason, checking the float and needle valve.

A sound plug which has been working at the right temperature in a good engine should have only slight deposits of a light brown or grey colour. The electrodes should not be worn and the tip of the insulator should be clean and light brown.

An oily plug may indicate that too cold a plug has been used (see the engine handbook for the correct specification) but more probably that the engine has been run for a while at low power or the fuel/oil mixture has had too much oil. This is especially likely if the fuel/oil mixture has been stored for some time, as the fuel tends to evaporate, leaving an excessive concentration of oil. Other possibilities are worn piston rings or cylinder bores.

A sooty carbon deposit is the sign of too rich a mixture (due to the carburettor setting or wrong operation of the choke), a weak spark, long periods of idling, too cold a plug, or a dirty air cleaner.

If the insulator is white or light grey and has small black or grey/brown spots, it indicates that the plug has been overheated and should be discarded. It's worth checking that the plug was of the right heat range, but more likely causes are ignition too far advanced, a weak mixture, the wrong grade of fuel, or general overheating of the engine.

More serious symptoms are electrodes that look melted, and blistered insulators. This can be caused by wrong ignition timing, too hot a plug, or general overheating.

Where plug trouble is identified, fit a spare set. The original plugs can then be either cleaned and adjusted, or if necessary replaced. Even if the plugs look in good condition, check the gap.

Checks of an outboard's ignition system follow the same lines as for petrol engines in general, but for a non-electric engine with conventional contact breaker ignition there is no voltage for a test lamp with the engine stationary, so a small battery has to be included in the test lamp circuit.

INDEX